Radical Rebirth

What They Said…

"A punch in the guts from a guy who's been on the canvas and come back up to the top. Randy Gage's *RADICAL REBIRTH* is a cohesive, no-bullshit philosophy packed as tight as a stick of dynamite. It's a cry of the heart, an in-your-face rant that made me rethink a bunch of assumptions I have long held dear."

– Steven Pressfield
Author of *The Legend of Bagger Vance,
Gates of Fire,* and *The War of Art*

"Damn, I love this book! Randy is a thought-leader who actually thinks. Just like a dirty air filter on your A/C unit impacts the quality of the air you breathe, a dirty life filter impacts the quality of life you live. Randy shows you how to change your filter!"

– Larry Winget
Six-time *New York Times/Wall Street Journal* bestselling author of *Shut Up, Stop Whining & Get a Life, You're Broke Because You Want to Be, Grow a Pair* and more.

"This book is not for the faint of heart! I haven't read a book this provocative for a long time and that is high praise. Gage's book isn't about right answers but asking the best questions to help you find out not who you are, but who you really want to be."

– Mark Sanborn
Author of *The Potential Principle*
and *The Intention Imperative*

"Yep, the 'Mad Genius' has done it again! What you will attain from the lessons in these pages is how (not what) to think much, much more productively, and a veritable road map for living a life of happiness, success, and abundance. Let's put it the way: If Ayn Rand's and Matt Ridley's books had a child...it would be the book you are holding in your hand (or seeing on the screen) right now. In other words, it would be filled with logic, premise-checking of long-held beliefs, and even a whole bunch of things you still disagree with. And that's okay."

– Bob Burg
Co-author of *The Go-Giver* book series

"With gleeful precision, Randy Gage ignores all the rules, AGAIN. *Radical Rebirth* plunges you into a mind stretch that challenges every single one of your beliefs. From unpacking burnout, to desiring significance, to claiming self-forgiveness, Gage takes you on an exquisite and often hysterical quest to shift from unconscious to conscious thinking. Buckle up for a wickedly smart, mind-bending ride."

– Dr. Shawne Duperon

"Just when I think I'm doing really well and playing a pretty great game, Randy Gage comes out with a new book. My reality is that I can't not read Randy Gage's new book, and every time I do, I realize that I'm not playing a great game at all. I'm playing small. Because no matter how much I achieve, Randy reminds me that there's more that I can experience, live, and be. Randy makes me so damned uncomfortable with myself. Which is why I can't not read Randy Gage's new book."

– Joe Calloway
Author of *Becoming a Category of One*

"You may not agree with his answers, but you can't afford to ignore his life questions! In this book, Randy Gage will challenge and encourage simultaneously."

– Barry Banther
Author of *A Leader's Gift – How to Earn the Right to be Followed*

"Randy Gage has written another mind-bending book. Whether you agree with him or disagree with him – and I do both regularly – he's always going to stretch your mind to the boundaries and challenge your commonly held beliefs so you can become all that you desire to be."

– Chris Widener
Author of *Lasting Impact: Creating a Life and Business That Lives Beyond You*

"*Radical Rebirth* is like the author who wrote it. Brash, thought-provoking, and more than a little confrontational. But if you've ever felt like you took the wrong turn or wanted a chance to reboot your life – this is the book for you."

– Dr. Nido R. Qubein
President, High Point University

"There are many factors that make up who we are today; however, where is it said that we have to follow that same predisposed path? As adults, we pave our own way but sometimes we need to break free from patterns that were programmed into our brains early on and take stock of our decisions. Randy's book provides the right 'anti-virus' to stop the malware that limits us. Read the book, be bold, take the leap, and experience the radical rebirth."

– Jeffrey Hayzlett
Primetime TV & Podcast Host, Speaker, Author and Part-Time Cowboy

"*Radical Rebirth* stretched my thinking so much that my brain hurt. Get ready to question everything and be slapped in the face with your own complacent mediocrity. You will be better for it."

– Randy Pennington
Author of *Make Change Work and Results Rule!*

"After 45 years of speaking and writing, I quit doing what I knew how to do and started doing things I didn't...it's a lot tougher. The safety of the platform was gone. When that happens and you're laid bare, you hear and understand hard things differently, more clearly. Especially during a rebirth. For me the book is perfect and perfectly timed – thanks, Randy."

– Ian Percy
Founder, Corrgenta Coding System LLC and the Senior Wellness Research Foundation

"A no-holds-barred call to action to rebirth yourself for freedom, prosperity, and abundance? Check. A powerful story of how to heal and forgive? Absolutely. A wake-up call, in the tradition of Randy's other books, for critical thinking, an end to victimhood, and reprogramming the scarcity out of your mind? You bet."

– Curt Mercadante
Bestselling author, *Five Pillars of the Freedom Lifestyle*

"Gage always writes with passion, vision, and great clarity. He has outdone himself with *Radical Rebirth*. It's a call to arms against everything in life that threatens to keep you small, shrinking in fear, and chained to a past full of self-loathing. Warning: Don't buy this book unless you are ravenously hungry for a complete life transformation."

– Louis Di Bianco
Award-nominated actor, acting coach and entrepreneur

Radical Rebirth

Kill off the old you and create a new life

RANDY GAGE

RUPA

Published by
Rupa Publications India Pvt. Ltd 2023
7/16, Ansari Road, Daryaganj
New Delhi 110002

Sales Centres:
Prayagraj Bengaluru Chennai
Hyderabad Jaipur Kathmandu
Kolkata Mumbai

Copyright © Randy Gage 2023

This translation published by arrangement with Columbine
Communications & Publications, Walnut Creek, California USA,
www.columbinecommunications.com

The views and opinions expressed in this book are the author's own and the facts
are as reported by her which have been verified to the extent possible, and the
publishers are not in any way liable for the same.

All rights reserved.
No part of this publication may be reproduced, transmitted,
or stored in a retrieval system, in any form or by any means,
electronic, mechanical, photocopying, recording or otherwise,
without the prior permission of the publisher.

P-ISBN: 978-93-5702-133-3
E-ISBN: 978-93-5702-134-0

First impression 2023

10 9 8 7 6 5 4 2 3 1

Printed in India

This book is sold subject to the condition that it shall not, by way of
trade or otherwise, be lent, resold, hired out, or otherwise circulated,
without the publisher's prior consent, in any form of binding or
cover other than that in which it is published.

Contents

Introduction
"You Don't Belong in Here. You Are Capable
of Great Things."   1

Chapter One
Recognizing When Your Life Sucks...   7

Chapter Two
You and the Zombie Ant   21

Chapter Three
Why You Love to Hate Rich People   37

Chapter Four
Alexa and Siri Are Coming for You...   63

Chapter Five
Blowing Up Bad Beliefs About Money
and Success   75

Chapter Six
Toxic Relationships Come from Toxic Beliefs   81

Chapter Seven
Celebrating Sex and Sexuality   89

Chapter Eight
Hope, Dope, and a Very Dead Pope   101

Chapter Nine
Could You Do Three Pull-Ups to Save
Your Life?   113

Chapter Ten
Rejecting False Identities   123

Chapter Eleven
Living in Divine Discontent   129

Chapter Twelve
Rebooting Your Operating System   137

Chapter Thirteen
Crafting Your Ideal Vision   149

Chapter Fourteen
Becoming the Thinker of the Thought   157

Chapter Fifteen
Beware of the Soul-Crushers   165

Chapter Sixteen
The Power of Forgiveness   173

Chapter Seventeen
A Rebirth Worthy of You   185

Recognizing Generosity   201

Introduction

"You Don't Belong in Here. You Are Capable of Great Things."

I WAS READY TO leave for school in my white jeans one day when my mom eyed me over and said, "You can't wear white after Labor Day." When I wanted to know the source or rationale for this indisputable decree, my poor, flummoxed mother didn't have an answer. People in the Midwest just follow these habits and customs; no one ever asks why.

Like me, you had formative experiences, a certain environment you were raised in, and hundreds if not thousands of mindless premises and foundational beliefs you were programmed with. All of those things led you in a certain direction, a pathway to the kind of life you were meant to live.

At least until you decide *that* life isn't supposed to be *your* life.

It's been said that before you tell your life what you intend to do with it, you should first listen to what it intends to do with you. That's probably not bad advice – to first ascertain the path you're being directed to.

But it's usually horrible advice to blindly accept that route without a little (or a lot of) introspection.

There are many people and external circumstances influencing that possible life: Your religion or lack of it, where you were born, your ethnicity, what political party is dominant in your area, how happy or unhappy your parents are, the schools you attend, and literally hundreds of other factors. Many of these influences are not designed for your highest good. And a fair number are downright destructive.

In my case, the path laid out for me was clear. I would eat clam chowder at Friday night fish fries, work the assembly line at the GM plant in Janesville, Wisconsin, and become a Green Bay Packer fan. Alas, I hate clams, mindless repetitive work, and ugly uniforms. (Not to mention despise cold weather.)

My formative years came during the anti-war movement, rioting in America, and the residual aftermath of Woodstock. I couldn't just forget I had witnessed all that and ease into the Midwestern life of bowling once a week, drinking Pabst Blue Ribbon, and visiting the Tommy Bartlett Water Show at Wisconsin Dells. By the time I reached 15 years old, I was in full rebellion mode. I became a teenage alcoholic and drug addict, feeling helpless and broke, furious with the world for keeping me down. I was enamored with the concept of socialism and decided to implement the redistribution personally, by committing a series of burglaries and armed robberies. As you might expect, this career path did not end well, and I soon found myself in jail awaiting trial.

"You Don't Belong in Here. You Are Capable of Great Things."

One day, unexpectedly, I heard the sound of jangling keys and then the lock turning in the cell door. In walked a blond stranger. He introduced himself as Baxter Richardson, a teacher and the father of my best friend's girlfriend. His daughter had beseeched him to visit me in jail to see if he could help me. I had a hard time believing the message he came to deliver. That message was...

"You don't belong in here. You are capable of great things."

When he told me that, I thought he was delusional. I figured if he knew anything about me, he would know I was a lost, troubled soul, one in the habit of making very poor decisions. But that wasn't the teenager he saw...

Baxter said, "I spoke with your teachers. They told me you skip class for weeks at a time, then come in and ace a test. Your reading comprehension is above college level. You don't belong in here. You are capable of great things."

Funny thing: I desperately wanted to believe him...and so I did. And because I believed him...what he said was true.

Do you really get that? And recognize that if I had believed the opposite – that I was a worthless fuckup beyond redemption – *that* would have been true instead? Think about what that means to you... the path you are given, and the path you ultimately choose to live.

With the help of many people – Baxter, my public defender, and others who believed in me – I was released on probation and given another chance. Which is really what this book is about. It's a breakdown of how you fight back, kill the old you, release that which no longer serves you, and evolve into the person you are meant to become.

I took a job and committed to becoming wealthy through hard work and integrity. Then at 17 years old, I packed everything I could fit into my '71 Plymouth and drove to Miami. I didn't have a place to stay, much less a job, and didn't know a single person there. But I had about 350 bucks and a dream to live somewhere that didn't include 60-below-zero wind-chill factors. I traded monster snowstorms for palm trees, ribeye steaks at the Elks Lodge for arroz con pollo on South Beach, and a North Face insulated coat for a Hugo Boss linen suit. Instead of dropping engines into Chevrolet Impalas, I chose a pathway that ultimately led to me writing these words to you.

It wasn't all seashells, balmy breezes, and drinking from coconuts...

I stayed in a roach-infested, hooker motel on Biscayne Boulevard for two months until I found a job and saved enough money to put down a security deposit on an apartment. Miami provided my first encounters with hurricanes, rain forest humidity, and getting shot by a crack addict. But I believe that decision to start over at 17 years old was the seminal moment in my lifetime: the moment I stopped tolerating life and started co-creating it.

Spiritual legends tell us of the Ashim. Although they are spoken of in numerous traditions and different languages, all definitions of the Ashim hold a similar theme: An endless, boundless being – someone who challenges limitations so as to embark on a journey of ongoing personal growth and development. When you choose to live in the way of the Ashim, you're not choosing so much to study and learn, but to seek and unfold. That's what we will explore together in this book: How to unleash your innate gifts – the mad genius that is uniquely yours. Although you will discover references to the Ashim in many religions, what I'm going to share with you is about as anti-religion as can be. There is a very practical and tangible objective here:

To become the highest possible version of yourself.

You don't become a success and live a prosperous life because you have no challenges. Or even fewer challenges than most people. You become successful by seeking out a continuous progression of escalating challenges – then doing the difficult work of trial, growth, and self-development to overcome them.

This means an exploration of the thoughts you allowed yourself to be influenced by (whether consciously or subconsciously), the beliefs they caused you to develop, and then what the results of holding those beliefs have been. This introspection and the accompanying critical thinking are important work – because they allow you to become conscious of the process, then mindfully direct it in a positive manner. This is the method that creates a radical rebirth. You can't have lasting, meaningful happiness unless you're willing to continually reinvent yourself. That reinvention always starts by challenging yourself.

When you make this choice, you really realize how monumentally insignificant Black Fridays, Instagram likes, BREAKING NEWS alerts, Monday-morning quarterback controversies, snarky tweets, and office politics really are. To become the highest possible version of yourself doesn't require renouncing your possessions, becoming an ascetic, or leaving your loved ones behind to join a monastery. (Unless you want to.) You don't have to shave your head, burn incense, or meditate in a cave. (Unless you want to.) You simply choose to consciously and mindfully practice self-development and personal growth...*to create a radical rebirth*.

The path already laid out for you may show you that you'll drive a Lexus, have a summer home on the lake, and become a successful dentist like your mother. And if that path feels right for you, by all means savor the journey.

But before you blindly go down the path the world has in store for you, you may want to do some serious critical thinking on whether that path will lead you to becoming the person you're meant to become – the one you truly desire to be.

To make that happen, you're going to have to be willing to let go of – or even kill off – the old you. To do that, we need to find out how you got to the state you are in right now. And that's where we will begin...

Randy Gage

Miami Beach, Fla.

November 2020

Chapter One

Recognizing When Your Life Sucks...

Put yourself in this picture:

You're staring down a Death Star which is powering up its beam to destroy your world. You're standing alone on the planet's surface, poised for battle, holding a steak knife. Believe it or not, that's an accurate analogy for the forces you have faced – and *almost* defeated – up to this point in your life. (And the reason you are almost certainly subconsciously doing behavior that is self-sabotaging your happiness and success.)

You might think I'm exaggerating. I'm not. Since you were a toddler, you have faced overwhelming forces determined to brainwash you, hold you down, destroy your self-esteem, manipulate you into buying shit you don't need, consuming toxic substances, going into debt, blowing up your relationships, and becoming a worker drone in the collective.

Most of you reading this have never met me in person, or perhaps we shared a quick handshake or a photo at a seminar. But I still know a couple very important things about you...

First, I know there were times in your life when a door slammed and you thought something was over, only to discover that a greater good was awaiting you through a different avenue. And second, I know that some of your greatest accomplishments sprouted from some of your most difficult challenges.

Are you the person you always dreamt of becoming, or did you settle for being someone else? Maybe you bought someone else's story for yourself. Or maybe you zigged when you should have zagged, and that led you down a path that took you to a world you never intended to live in. The fact that you're reading this book is a pretty good indication that you may be writing a story that isn't really yours. Or perhaps you woke up one day and realized you simply don't like (or even hate) the person you have become. In either case, that doesn't have to be a bad thing. In fact, it may be a wonderful development.

Because every failure you have endured, every obstacle you have overcome, and every challenge you have conquered has made you stronger, wiser, and better prepared for your true destiny. These stepping stones were necessary. Because without them you could never discover, understand, and take action on the path you need to travel from this point forward. You were too ignorant, too arrogant – or both – to be able to receive the message your life has been sending you about yourself. Don't beat yourself up over that. You've suffered enough, paid your penance, served your time. You have grown in consciousness. Release the old you, forgive yourself, and move forward to accept your abundance.

Don't let who you have been prevent you from being who you can become.

Sometimes version 1.0 of the software isn't the one that works in the market. (And sometimes neither does version 2.0 or 3.0.) But as long as you're willing to keep fixing bugs and making upgrades, you eventually get to the version that works. And that's what this delicious experience we call life is really about. The journey of unfolding into the person you are truly meant to be.

Best case scenario, this is simply a matter of releasing the old you. But if you've been acting out deeply ingrained, intergenerational toxic patterns – it may require killing off the old you.

Some may tell you this is a years-long process. They might suggest you need to quantify your unmet childhood needs, search for repressed feelings and memories, or get in touch with your inner child. You can take five years with a psychiatrist and go through the Rorschach ink blots, search for the meaning of symptoms, perform dream analysis, and question all your many instances of parapraxes, resistance, transference, and panic attacks. (And maybe you should. I had four years of therapy and found it extremely helpful.) But whether you work with a mental health counselor or not, you don't have to wait to find the right therapist to make a change in your life. I believe the best advice is the simplest. So let's keep this simple:

If your life sucks, it's not the life you were meant to live. Change it.

You don't have to be in denial or shame about living a sucky life. There is no need to succumb to depression and resigned acceptance. Millions of people were programmed to make the same mistakes you did. Simply having this realization is 80 percent of the breakthrough. Once you do, you can make the decision to stop living the old life and start creating a new one. Be willing to let go of who you are now and transform into who you are meant to become.

The most liberating day of your life is the day you realize that some bridges are meant to be burned.

There are some beliefs, habits, and even people, that no longer belong in your life. Once you realize and recognize this reality, you can finally give yourself permission to move on. Then you get a second chance at a clean canvass on which to paint your life. (In some cases, this is actually your first chance.) Now your journey of self-mastery can truly begin. But first you have to recognize the sheer scope and scale of the forces that have been working to hold you down, as well as acknowledge what an extraordinary job you've done just by still hanging on (even if only barely) at this particular moment in the space/time continuum.

If you're going to retire or kill off the old you, it's important that you understand how you became that person, to uncover those formative elements that led you astray. Let's break down what this looks like...

We all have developed core foundational beliefs about the world around us and how we fit into it. The most important core beliefs, in terms of the self-esteem you develop and how happy and successful you ultimately become, can be quantified in the following six categories:

- ▶ Money/Success
- ▶ Marriage/Relationships
- ▶ Sex/Sexuality
- ▶ God/Religion
- ▶ Health/Wellness
- ▶ Career/Work

Here's a frightening, startling, and yet extremely cogent fact: Your default setting on most or all of these beliefs was set before you were 10 years old. Really. (For most of these, before you reached the age of seven.)

Did your parents affirm things like "money doesn't grow on trees" and "we can't afford that?" You probably had feelings of jealousy (or even hate) for wealthy people before you were six.

Did one of your parents cheat on the other, or did they argue all of the time as you were growing up? You crystallized core beliefs about marriage and romantic relationships before you ever experienced your first one.

Was sex a taboo subject in your home growing up? Were you taught conventional beliefs like boys play with trucks and become doctors and girls play with dolls and become nurses? You were a mess of hang-ups, gender bias, and dysfunctional sexual beliefs before you even reached puberty.

Did the nuns in your Catechism class rap your knuckles with a ruler and teach that you were born a sorry sinner? Your core beliefs about god and religion were pretty much set by the time you were six.

As a child, was 90 percent of the food in your pantry manufactured substances like breakfast cereals, frozen entrees, and pastas with an expiration date a couple years in the future? Did the role models in your life carry an extra five pounds for every decade older they were? Did your grandparents (or even parents) have 10 different prescriptions they took daily? If so, you developed some very limiting beliefs about health and wellness before you were a teenager.

Were you taught that work was something to be endured for eight hours a day, and then you live your life only after putting in your time? Or that working for a big company or becoming a union member would provide financial security for your family? Either way you bought into a lie.

You may think it's a far-fetched idea that beliefs you developed in these six areas are dramatically impacting your relationships, prosperity, and happiness decades later, but that reality is pretty much a given. You could be sabotaging your marriage, getting passed up for a promotion, or have $50,000 worth of credit card debt right now – because of programming you received at six, seven, or eight years old. Really.

The suffocating and overpowering forces used against you weren't employed on a public battlefield, but in the unseen reaches of your subconscious mind. You have been brainwashed without your knowledge. Since your formative years you've been exposed to dysfunctional, limiting, and even dangerous memes.

The term "meme" has been hijacked and is frequently used to describe a slide on social media, but that's not what we're discussing here. This word was first coined by Richard Dawkins in his book, *The Selfish Gene*. Dawkins took the Greek root of "mimeme" and shortened it to meme, to be more suggestive of gene. A meme is a mind virus – an idea that is also a replicator. Think of a meme as something that causes people to think a certain way, believe a particular thing, or take a specific action – much like genes do. A catchy jingle or slogan is a meme. You hear it, you play it in your head, and then you "infect" other minds by sharing it. "Just do it" and "Yes we can" are memes as are the *Baby Shark* theme song and the idea that rich people are evil. A meme complex (or memeplex) is a condition of mutually supporting memes that form a belief system.

Just as your laptop hard drive can get infected with a virus from an email, your subconscious mind can be infected with a mind virus from the environment around you. That's exactly what's happened in the examples above. The result of being infected with mind viruses like those is self-sabotage.

Here's what that looks like: You want something with your conscious mind, but you have a core belief in your subconscious mind that is sabotaging you from achieving that goal. An example is the millions, perhaps billions of people who are more afraid of success than they are of failure. They're self-sabotaging themselves and have no idea they are doing it.

Why?

Because they don't realize they got programmed with these mind viruses and then developed negative and dysfunctional beliefs from them. They blame their less-than-desirable results on the government, their cheap boss, the economy, their spouse, or their ex. (Or frequently, all of the above.) They're convinced the cause is some outside circumstance, not realizing that the call is coming from inside the house.

Go to the barrios of San Salvador and you will witness thousands of people living lifestyles of meager subsistence. They toil very long hours (in difficult tasks like scrubbing bathrooms, working in construction, or washing dishes), sleep, then arise to do it all over again. It's easy to feel empathy for them, believing they are helpless pawns going through life in an almost comatose state.

Yet when I drink in the view from my penthouse apartment in Miami Beach and see all my neighbors in their expensive island homes, I realize that most of them are living in a similar oblivion. Sure, they're driving BMWs, shopping in Bal Harbor, and have a premium package with Showtime, Disney+, and Netflix. But they're still worker drones in the collective – living a life devoid of self-awareness.

They don't know this of course. Because the people in the Matrix never realize they're in the Matrix…

An overwhelming majority of people are mindlessly being jerked on puppet strings and have no idea. He's the rancher who fears black and brown people and doesn't know it's because he watches FOX News at night. She's the corporate HR director who thinks she's hungry again at 9 pm but doesn't understand it's because she's been exposed to more than 20 fast-food commercials during her evening television viewing. He's the broke wannabe entrepreneur who swipes up on Instagram to buy yet another get-rich-quick e-book.

Each of these people believes they are free thinkers and independent beings, because they have surrounded themselves with people who buy their stories. But these stories are created and nurtured by the mind viruses in the collective consciousness. Remember this scene from *The Matrix?*

Agent Smith: Do we have a deal, Mr. Reagan?

Cypher: You know, I know this steak doesn't exist. I know that when I put it in my mouth, the Matrix is telling my brain that it is juicy and delicious. After nine years, you know what I realize? Ignorance is bliss…

That scene is the perfect analogy to demonstrate that the actual role of collective consciousness is to keep people unconscious. That's because what we call society is just a collection of people. And when you assemble a large collection of people, you can be certain that a vast majority of them are living out knee-jerk reactions based on the memes they are infected with. Most are unhappy, unhealthy, deeply in debt, and even deeper in denial and delusion.

You want to feel loved and accepted. The advertising agencies that peddle soda, beer, and snack foods know exactly how to emotionally manipulate you to feel that way. And if they can emotionally manipulate you into that first purchase, then their products are designed to cause physical addiction afterward. Queso-flavored tortilla chips taste better than squash because they are genetically engineered to do so. But which one actually provides you nutrients?

You can be a powerless failure, living in your mom's basement. But the social media networks allow you to feel powerful by creating a psychological avatar, where you can insult, avenge, troll, and irritate people until you're noticed. Every retweet, share, and reply will feed this superficial sense of control.

Ultimately, this is a game you can only lose...

You sacrifice and go into debt to get a status brand car, but your neighbor buys a higher status one. You haven't paid the credit card debt from your last iPhone before Apple releases the next model. You're confident you've found the next trendy Merlot and then your hipster neighbor announces the new IPA he's discovered. If you play fucked up games you win fucked up prizes.

Let me break some sad news to you:

▶ Your sex life will not be like those porno movies you've watched. Off the set, those porno stars are wondering what they can do to spice up their own sex life.

▶ More followers on Facebook or Instagram will not make you happier. It will only create the pressure of trying to convince yet more people that you are happy.

▶ Having six people lusting after your body will not make you feel secure. On a deeper level, you know that looks are superficial and transitory.

▶ Likewise, you can get breast or pec implants, undergo a nose job, and Botox away all of your wrinkles. You are still you, and the value and worth with which you hold yourself will not change, because you know that the genuine you underneath the veneer hasn't changed.

▶ You will not be as sage, charming, and kind as the characters on your favorite sitcom. That shit is make-believe, all scripted by writers possessed by their own self-sabotage memes.

The common denominator in all these scenarios is a futile attempt to find self-worth from external factors. And your self-worth can never come from things outside of yourself – that has to come from the inside.

All of this pursuit of status and superficial acceptance can leave you feeling lonely, directionless, and empty. You seek something bigger than yourself to be a part of. Then it's likely that a gang, cult, or organized religion will offer you a place and a process to disguise that feeling of emptiness. Or you will collect college degrees, titles, and awards, desperate to feel worthy. Or you try to assuage your emptiness with copious consumption or drown it out with drugs and alcohol.

Please pause and take a deep breath before you read the next paragraph...

I am not joking about living in the Matrix. Because you really are living in a Matrix; it's just not configured like the one in the movies. The real Matrix is a collection of machines used for surveillance and data-gathering. (This includes every online search you perform, what you buy, every website you visit, your social media posts, the things you ask your voice assistants, the apps running in the background on your phone, and what you stream for entertainment.) Then this data is exploited to manipulate your habits, moods, identity, beliefs, and behaviors. The objectives are to make you feel powerless, needy, and helpless – and drive you to take self-destructive actions that reward the managers of the Matrix.

The damaging results to humans are not debatable. They're on display daily in society all around you. They include:

- ▶ Low self-esteem
- ▶ Loss of free will
- ▶ Fear-based decision-making
- ▶ Increasing levels of depression and suicides

- Shortened attention spans
- Inability for critical thinking
- Growing polarization

You will always be a slave to whatever you're unaware of. It doesn't matter if we're talking about people, institutions, customs, habits, programming, or emotions. The only real freedom comes from self-awareness.

And that's what we will explore next...

Chapter Two

You and the Zombie Ant

THERE IS AN Ophiocordyceps fungus which invades an ant's exoskeleton, forcing the ant to climb a tree and bite onto a twig – an act of suicide that results in its head exploding and raining down more fungus spores on the ants below, who repeat the process. Essentially, the fungal pathogen infects the ant, causing it to kill itself and perpetuate a reflexive cycle of zombie ants ravaging the colony.

If you're wondering if I am saying the reason you buy a Lexus, become addicted to cocaine, or support a particular political party is because you've been taken over like a zombie ant – I would never insult your intelligence by suggesting...well, come to think of it, yeah, that's pretty much what I am saying.

For my money, the most insightful observation Freud ever made was that until you make the unconscious conscious, you'll call it fate. We all have a "command center" (subconscious mind) that governs our behavior. Think of it like the main computer on the bridge of the Starship Discovery. Either you write the software for the computer, or you just accept the preinstalled software it came with. If you choose the latter, the code someone else wrote controls your behavior, based on whatever mind viruses it has been programmed with. In this case, that software is your subconscious mind.

If you have many of the subconscious memes that most people do – money is evil, rich people are corrupt, you were born a sorry sinner requiring penance, etc. – your command center causes you to self-sabotage your success. When you bring those subconscious mind viruses and limiting beliefs into the light, you develop self-awareness and those mind viruses lose their power over you. Only then can you run the command center. Which leads us back to the question of whether you're running your command center or being controlled like the zombie ant. Are you able to objectively and rationally process information that challenges your core beliefs? And how can you avoid reacting in a knee-jerk manner, personalizing the issue, or jumping the shark?

Here's the thing we must all be aware of, and fight against, all the time...

Each of us processes all that we experience through our own personal filters. This is especially true with what we see and hear. For example, let's suppose there is a workout video on YouTube. If I watch it, I'm going to filter it through a prism of how the routine portrayed might help me extend my legendary (in my own mind) career as a softball player. Someone with a bad back might view it in terms of how it could reduce their sciatica, another person who is overweight might look at the workout for the fat-burning potential, and a marathon runner would be interested in how it could help their endurance. It's the same video, but we would all view it through our unique filters. Whether each of us "like" or share the video would depend on how it relates to our particular predisposition toward the subject. Which is another way of saying we all will view the video with our unique confirmation bias. Then there's a common practice that takes our confirmation bias to a higher level of dysfunction: assigning labels to yourself. I will propose the following premise to begin the discussion:

Every time you apply a label to yourself, you incrementally lower your IQ.

Because once you brand yourself with a label – you have created an identity for yourself. And once you create an identity for yourself – it's human nature to instinctively, impulsively, and unconsciously defend that identity.

Any time you are acting instinctively, impulsively, and unconsciously, you have reduced your ability for rational and critical thought. While you haven't technically lowered your IQ, you have for all practical purposes locked a portion of it into a vault you're unable to access. And if you can't access that intelligence, it's no more helpful than not having it to begin with. Essentially, every time you decide to add another label to yourself, it's an elective lobotomy.

Let's say you spent three weeks on research before you bought your new car. You were even able to get a VIP tour of the Lexus factory and were so persuaded that you bought one. Deliriously happy and excited, you called all of your friends and posted pix on social media. You've now identified as a proud Lexus owner. Six months later, your neighbor comes home raving about the new BMW she just bought. You will instinctively feel compelled to defend the benefits of your Lexus. In fact, that BMW could have 25 features that make it superior to your car, but you won't even be able to process that information – until you stop identifying yourself as a proud Lexus owner. This is human nature.

It doesn't matter how simple, harmless, or even noble you believe the label is...

Even if you think the label is a good one – such as scholar or philanthropist or Christian – the simple process of identifying yourself by that label will cloud your rational judgment. Your need to protect your identity conflicts with your ability for logical, rational thought.

You will find that people who are infected with too many mind viruses, or have been indoctrinated with them since early childhood, sometimes cannot be reasoned with. I don't write the following paragraph to be mean, snarky, or controversial. It simply is what it is.

There is no reasoning with such people. They are essentially brainwashed and are not capable of rational, logical thought in areas where they have been programmed with memes. They can be highly successful functioning adults, even have a high level of intelligence. But in these areas, they are completely oblivious to how irrational, illogical, even crazy their thinking may be.

To debate a topic with those people who are subconsciously programmed with such mind viruses would be akin to attempting a thoughtful conversation with Donald Trump. (Or anyone with a similar level of insecurity or narcissism.) In Trump's case, it isn't memes that block his rational thinking abilities, but his narcissistic personality disorder. He's unable to follow the logical progression of any discussion because the "filters" through which he hears all information relate only to himself and his insecurities. Any attempt at a coherent conversation will end up something like this:

You: Mr. President, do you think it's going to be sunny this July?

Trump: I like sun. I've always liked sunny days ever since I was growing up. I like sun. I like sunny days. I was at my golf resort last week and it was a beautiful, sunny day. It was a sunny day like no one has ever seen. In fact, many people are saying my resort is the sunniest resort in the country, maybe the world.

You: I was asking if you thought it was going to be sunny in July.

Trump: I like July too. July has always been a good month for me. I cut the ribbon for one of my Trump Towers in July one year.

You: Never mind. Do you think Ford is going to offer the new electric Mustang in purple?

Trump: I love purple. Purple is one of my favorite colors. I love purple. I love purple a lot. I was just saying to Melania how much I like purple. She gave me a purple bathrobe for my birthday...

Watch mindfully when Trump is interviewed. You will see that it doesn't matter what question is asked, what the topic is, or how many times it is repeated – he is incapable of delivering any other answer than one about himself. Unfortunately, many people who have wrapped their primary identity around a label (Muslim, conservative, vegetarian, etc.) also have the same inability to follow a logical progression of thought in a discussion.

While you're interacting with people in your world, you're going to encounter many who are so infected with mind viruses, they will have a similar inability to follow rational, logical thought. Buying into their craziness is not going to make your life easier, even though it seems like the path of lesser resistance. You have to immunize yourself against irrationality because it leads to bad decisions which create a life below what you are meant to live.

In the case of this book, I'm writing it through the filter of an author (label/identity I assign myself) – creating a book that can help people identify limiting beliefs and replace them with empowering ones. I pride myself on my critical thinking ability (label/identity I assign myself), so the goal is to write a book for open-minded "big kids" (label/identity I assign to others), not one pandering to people wallowing in victimhood (label/identity I assign to others).

Whole lotta filters going on here...

You and the Zombie Ant

One way to neutralize your filters is by becoming a participant/observer. When you make the jump to participant/observer, you're up at 30,000 feet, able to objectively watch the tug-of-war between your conscious and subconscious minds. This entails developing the self-awareness to debug and reprogram your subconscious mind – recognizing any limiting beliefs and replacing them with empowering ones.

When you possess self-awareness, you're not easily manipulated because you're always in a dual role of participant and observer. (Running the command center.) When you hear something that creates cognitive dissonance with a core belief you have, you pause, question the premise, do some critical thinking, and reach a conclusion. You may change your original belief, or you may keep that belief, but at least you have exposed your belief to subjective questioning.

- ▶ You can read a scathing political diatribe in your Facebook feed and instead of attacking the author, you can recognize the mind viruses that caused them to act that way.

- ▶ You can enjoy that Corona beer commercial of sexy people in skimpy swimsuits frolicking on the beach and still be thinking, "Funny that no one has a beer belly."

- ▶ You can watch Fox News because you desire a conservative viewpoint, or MSNBC because you desire a liberal viewpoint, yet still recognize you're being exposed to a level of propaganda that Joseph Goebbels could only dream of.

- ▶ You can follow a Kardashian on Instagram to see what's trending in pop culture and also recognize that doing so makes you a product being sold to advertisers.

It takes a staggering level of critical thinking, intellectual capability, and self-awareness to be able to view your own opinions and beliefs – and, most importantly, how you reached them – objectively. If you're up for the challenge, here is what may be the key to your breakthrough in all of this...

When your conscious mind and subconscious mind have a conflict – the subconscious mind always wins.

Always. The only way you will end self-sabotage and improve your results is to identify the core, foundational, *subconscious* beliefs you possess that are negative, toxic, and dysfunctional. Then you must eviscerate those beliefs and replace them with beliefs that are positive, healthy, and empowering.

To accomplish this successfully, we need to first identify the source of the mind viruses. There are literally millions of triggers to this pandemic. But they can be categorized into four groups that create the vast majority of the damage. They are:

1. The Education System
2. Government
3. Organized Religion
4. The Datasphere

Let's break down each category and their potential for harming you. One important note: You won't find a "pro vs. con" breakdown of these four institutions. There are *many* benefits we can receive from education, government, religion, and the forces that make up the Datasphere. I'm not highlighting them here because: a) There are far better people than I who can (and do) make the case for them; and, b) This book isn't meant to study the merits of these four institutions. It is my viewpoint on what it takes to create a rebirth, and what obstacles have to be overcome to do so. So please don't take my criticisms on these institutions to mean I want them eliminated. I don't. If it seems I'm over-indexing on their negative practices, I am – simply because of the central tenet of this book: There are forces influencing your beliefs that could cause you to self-sabotage your health, happiness, and prosperity.

When something is based on a bad premise, everything that springs from that premise will be bad. Sadly, the education system is based on numerous bad premises. The most egregious of these are:

▶ Teaching kids what to think instead of how to think.
▶ Curriculum centered around memorizing facts.
▶ Teaching to pass tests instead of gaining knowledge.
▶ Failure to set curriculum applicable to practical living.

- ▶ Training worker drones instead of educating humans.

Because the education system impacts people at such a young age, it's a huge influence on creating lifetime limiting beliefs for billions of people. (Your years in school – from preschool through twelfth grade – are when you are your most malleable, impressionable, and vulnerable. And we can argue that for many people, their college years also played an instrumental role in shaping their thinking.)

The primary structural failure of education is that it doesn't teach the most fundamental skill to creating a prosperous life: the ability for critical thinking. Critical thinking is necessary to employ discernment to process information, analyze problems to create solutions, and, most importantly, become a free thinker. The current education system is designed to beat those traits and abilities out of people.

Then, by way of collateral damage, the vast majority of the teachers, advisors, professors, coaches, and guidance counselors are unknowingly programmed with the mind viruses we mentioned earlier. These well-meaning education professionals reinforce the limiting beliefs you developed at home throughout your formative years. If you were able to experience the educational system from kindergarten through college and don't currently reside in a mental hospital, homeless shelter, or penitentiary – you've already achieved a considerable victory.

As for governments, they can be categorized into two types:

1. Single-person/party rule. (Theocracies, autocracies, dictatorships, etc.)
2. Multiple-party rule (Democracies, federations, republics, etc.)

Whenever a single person or party holds all power, that power ultimately corrupts. You end up with dictators and despots, and the end result is anti-humanity and thus anti-prosperity. In the cases of multi-party rule, history has shown that inevitably this whittles down to two main parties. Then you have one party in power that wants to remain in power, and one party out of power, desperate to regain power. The inherent flaw in the two-party system comes from the universal law that the only free cheese is in the mousetrap.

Each party feeds into a competition to see who can offer the most "free cheese" in order to remain in or regain power. They ultimately disintegrate into dictatorships, communism, or socialism (which is simply communism with lipstick). These government models all kill free enterprise and individual initiative, so the end result is anti-humanity and thus anti-prosperity. As a result, governments can never create prosperity. At their very best, they can only facilitate it. The majority of the time, they kill it.

Most of the people who serve in government consciously want to do well for the people they serve. (Or at least they begin that way.) Unfortunately, this altruistic streak leads too many of them to believe they know how to take care of you better than you do yourself. Most importantly, to remain in power, *governments need you to need them*. To continue being viable, they must create entitlement and dependence, which are prosperity killers. While governments frequently promise to (and may actually desire to) liberate people, they ultimately enslave them.

Like most of the people in government, the majority of people involved in organized religion are also well-meaning. (Or at least they begin that way.) Similar to the zombie ants, they don't realize *they* are infected with the very memes they're programming you with. One of the sneakiest things about memes is they parasitize the host and cause it to unknowingly perpetuate the meme.

Religious memes are deeply centered in self-worth (or, more specifically, the lack of it), with most religions advocating that you are pitiful, unworthy, undeserving, or even inherently evil, in need of redemption. Whether we look at the Christian concept of original sin, the Buddhist Eightfold Path, the Hindu doctrine of karma, the Jewish Covenant, or the Muslim Code of Law – they are all set up with the basic presupposition that you are a flawed being needing salvation.

If, as a child, you were taught that you were born a sorry sinner, aren't worthy, are meant to suffer in this lifetime, won't reach enlightenment until another 44 lifetimes, or you've been reincarnated in this lifetime to pay penance for a past lifetime – it's a pretty safe bet that you'll grow into adulthood with low self-esteem and worthiness issues. The destructive results of this mind virus are heightened when combined with another meme from organized religion: the central tenet promoting that you are meant to suffer here to demonstrate your worthiness for the afterlife (when supposedly, the really good stuff comes). Programming like this frequently leads to self-sabotage behavior in your health, relationships, and career.

Essentially, these religions are operating cosmic "frequent flier" programs. If you acquire enough points (for the stuff you do or don't do) in this lifetime, you qualify for the award (salvation, nirvana, reincarnation, 72 virgins, eternal life, heaven, etc.). Depending on the religion, you can earn enough qualifying points if you prostrate yourself enough, beg for forgiveness enough, say enough Hail Marys, ambush enough American soldiers, rub enough rosary beads, pray enough, fly enough planes into skyscrapers, blow up enough abortion clinics, kill enough Jews, or send enough money to the televangelist. Personally, I prefer to take my chances trading in my miles to Delta for an award trip to Hawaii, rather than hoping for eternal life from a televangelist on an infomercial, but that's just me.

Religious proponents would make the case that religion provides inspiration and hope, and certainly that is true for many. The problems arise from some religious recruiting tactics that over-index on the unworthiness propaganda and tantalize you with redemption. This has produced hundreds of millions of people who believe they will receive their salvation only if they accept that they are inherently flawed, undeserving, and unworthy. If you fall prey to this programming, you doubt your abilities and set lower goals. You pass up opportunities that could advance you. And if you overcome this somehow and begin to become healthy, happy, or wealthy – you will probably subconsciously self-sabotage yourself.

These three sources of mind viruses we've discussed have been sowing harm and havoc for centuries. They were held in check by the good forces on the other side: ambition, empathy, hope, and a desire for our children to have better opportunities than their parents. But as communication developed, that allowed memes to infect more people, more quickly. Newspapers, magazines, and radio started tipping the scale towards the dark side. As major movie studios evolved and television gained acceptance, negative memes began winning the war in certain areas. Now there has been another development, one that has tipped the balance of power in the war to negative memes.

The Internet.

The Internet did not alter the balance of power by itself. But it allowed a whole new category of weapons of mass destruction to be developed: cable TV, streaming services, smart phones, mobile apps, podcasts, blogs, and e-gaming. These new tech weapons, working together with the ones developed in the earlier decades have become what we'll call the Datasphere.

We'll define the Datasphere to include TV, radio, blogs, movies, books, magazines, podcasts, newsletters, and now of course, social media. These are powerful, pervasive mediums and the more you are exposed to them (basically 24/7 for most people), the more potential mind viruses can program your subconscious mind.

The Datasphere provides an omnipotent multiplier effect to all of the limiting mind viruses perpetuated by the education system, governments, and organized religion. It is the Death Star for prosperity.

And how do you defeat a Death Star? By learning its design flaws. Which is what we'll attempt next...

Chapter Three

Why You Love to Hate Rich People

Have you ever reflected back on one of your previous relationships and had the thought: That was the one. Truly my soulmate. And I blew it.

Or have you ever had a dream job and either quit it or found a way to get fired from it?

Did you have a brilliant breakthrough idea for a business or product but didn't act on it – only to later see someone else make it a hit?

Were you ever powerless over an addiction, even though you knew it was destroying you?

Have you ever done something horrific to someone you loved, something that you desperately wish you could take back, but you can't?

If you've never experienced any of these five scenarios, you can close this book now and gift it to someone else. (Then please write your own book so I can buy it.) But if you have created one or more of these scenarios (or as I have, all five), we need to dig into this.

Why? Why do we take actions we know with every fiber of our being are foolish, hurtful, or even dangerous?

In almost every case, it's because we've got negative programming on the subconscious level that is overriding what we think we want on the conscious level. We are like those zombie ants. It is self-sabotage, plain and simple.

Last chapter I introduced the concept of the Datasphere and equated it to the Death Star for prosperity. Perhaps you were repelled by that imagery, thinking I'm being too alarmist or melodramatic. I am not.

Because now with the Datasphere, all of those negative, limiting, and destructive mind viruses you received from the education system, government, and organized religion get focused, amplified, and supercharged to program you for self-harm.

Because of the scope, swiftness, and power of the Datasphere, a meme that might have taken six years to traverse around the world in 1955 can now reach several billion people in a matter of days. The most insidious quality of mind viruses is how they infect then parasitize the host to replicate the viruses into the people around them. The Datasphere creates an endless loop of replication, creating "memeplexes" that continue to reinforce and propagate the viruses at the speed of the Internet.

The negative thought patterns created by the education system have been going on for at least a century or two. The helpless, needy, and entitlement mindsets governments and organized religion often use to manipulate their followers have been practiced for literally thousands of years. Now with the advent of our modern Datasphere, you are being assaulted with a digital tsunami of negative, toxic, and destructive mind viruses 24 hours a day.

For the first time in human history, we evolve more from the selection of adaptive ideas than biological hereditary traits. Meaning, memes are winning over genes. We do more because of mind viruses than DNA. A few decades of programming is overriding thousands of years of evolutionary development. In the war between a healthy future vision for humankind versus self-destructive behavior pulling us down, we are losing the war.

Because this war is fought against children...

Wars are won or lost on real estate, by taking (or defending) and occupying territory. In the case of mind viruses, the real estate is the subconscious minds of children. The tipping point is reached by adulthood.

You've probably heard analogies about ships or airplanes traveling great distances and how the final destination can fluctuate wildly if the course is off only by a degree or two. For you, your destination in life will fluctuate wildly depending on the state of your mental health by the time you cross into adulthood. The determining factors will be the levels of your:

- ▶ Confidence
- ▶ Optimism

- Self-Esteem
- Vision

Let's suppose child A reaches age 18 or 20 with confidence in her abilities, positive self-esteem, and an optimistic vision for her future. Wouldn't you rate her chances of achieving a healthy, happy, prosperous life pretty high?

Let's suppose child B reaches age 18 or 20 doubtful of his abilities, with negative self-esteem and a pessimistic view of his future. Wouldn't you rate his chances of achieving a healthy, happy, prosperous life pretty low?

Here are the most widespread memes being disseminated in the world today by the education system, government, and organized religion:

- You are not worthy.
- Money is bad.
- Rich people are evil.
- You have to sell your soul for money.
- You don't deserve to be healthy, happy, and rich.
- If you sacrifice now, you'll be rewarded in an afterlife.
- It's noble or spiritual to be poor.
- Companies have to be exploitative to be successful.
- You are not meant to be happy in this lifetime.

- To become successful requires being a bad parent.

Now through the power of the Datasphere, you are receiving literally hundreds of these negative memes every day. They're coming at you not only on a conscious level, but through subliminal, subconscious pathways as well. There you are, standing alone on the beach, holding that steak knife. To defeat the Death Star, you've got to find a design flaw. You need a similar approach to win against mind viruses.

As is true in most folklore, our superstitions and delusions, memes or mind viruses are most effectively spread by storytelling. These mind viruses are inadvertently embedded in the stories we tell ourselves: television, plays, opera, literature, movies, blogs, newscasts, editorials and op-eds, and virtually all mass communication. Let's break down how this plays out...

If you're old enough to have been around when the superhero movie trend took off, you probably bought some popcorn and a ticket to the original *Spiderman* movie. There's a part when his uncle says to Peter Parker/Spiderman, "We may not be rich, but at least we're honest."

What really happened as you watched that scene?

You probably thought you were simply gorging on some Milk Duds, enjoying a flick at your local cineplex. But what really went down is you were exposed to numerous limiting mind viruses, and they became implanted even more deeply into your subconscious mind. Have you ever thought through what an expression like the one above *really* means?

Let's translate it...

When Peter's uncle said, "We may not be rich, but at least we're honest," what he was really saying was, "Money is bad and rich people are evil. Be very glad that we are not rich, because that means we are good, noble, salt-of-the-earth people." And in today's Datasphere you are receiving subliminal messages like these on a nonstop basis. But before we get into that, you should know something else about mind viruses...

The more emotional they are, the faster they spread and the stronger their effect on you. As a result, any meme involving children or defenseless victims has mega power. Think about that *Spiderman* scene: Why was Peter's uncle raising him? Because poor Peter lost his parents; he is an orphan. When you are exposed to a protagonist who is an orphan, your emotional strings are played and the story (and underlying mind viruses) have a stronger impact on you. And it would appear being an orphan is a worldwide pandemic in the stories we tell each other. Take a quick look at the following list of orphans in fiction, particularly children's stories:

Tarzan
Snow White
Huckleberry Finn

- Tom Sawyer
- James Bond
- Captain America
- Heidi
- The Boxcar Children
- Mowgli
- Dorothy Gale (*Wizard of Oz*)
- Pied Piper
- Little Orphan Annie
- Hawkeye (Marvel)
- David Copperfield
- Po (*Kung Fu Panda*)
- Poison Ivy
- Batman
- Robin
- Lara Croft (*Tomb Raider*)
- Finn (*Star Wars*)
- Han Solo
- Anakin Skywalker
- Luke and Leia Skywalker
- Rey Skywalker
- The Mandalorian
- Worf (*Star Trek*)
- Michael Burnham (*Star Trek Discovery*)
- Cinderella
- Martin Brundle (*The Fly*)
- Frodo Baggins

- Superman
- Supergirl
- Firefly (DC Comics)
- Harry Potter
- Black Manta
- Daredevil
- Green Hornet
- Oliver Twist
- Professor X
- Wolverine
- Magneto
- Cyclops
- John Wick
- Jon Snow
- Daenerys Targaryen
- Pretty much anyone with the surname of Stark

Does that list just blow your mind? There are certain archetypal characters who emerge over and over throughout storytelling history, and a child without one or especially both parents is at the top of the list. As you can see above, not having parents seems to be the rule for heroes and superheroes. Lots of other protagonists appear to have lost their parents and been taken in by others. If the new family is cruel (Harry Potter and Cinderella) the power of the meme is boosted even more. Likewise, if our poor lonely orphans are left to fend for themselves (Mowgli, Oliver Twist, and the Boxcar Children).

You might think it's a sinister conspiracy undertaken by a secret cabal of Hollywood writers. The real cause of this situation is quite simple: If you're a screenwriter, you want to write a screenplay like the movies that impacted you the most. If you're an author, you want to write a book like the ones that spoke to you.

Simply put, the writers subconsciously followed the formula: They were exposed to mind viruses, got infected and parasitized by them, and then continued the spread of those mind viruses. And that, boys and girls and non-binaries, is how memes take over the world.

Now, if the predominant memes circulating were simply heroic stories of orphans overcoming the loss of their parents, perhaps we'd simply be inspired. Or the same might be true if the majority of memes suggested you are worthy and meant to be healthy, happy, and prosperous. But those are not the kind of memes gaining mass circulation...

You are being fed mostly negative memes – in a conscious, subconscious, or unconscious way – literally hundreds of times every day of your life. The Datasphere disseminates them through pop culture. In the '60s, '70s and '80s, books were still strong agents of cultural evolution, but television was the primary driver. By the '90s and aughts, books were waning, TV still was a major factor, but big studio movies began to play a larger role. Today, TV and movies still are huge cultural influencers, but blogs, social media, and other Internet-driven platforms are shaping societal programming (brainwashing) in a powerful way.

Radical Rebirth

> **Tell me what generation you are, and I can not only list the predominant cultural entertainment of your era, but demonstrate the evil, insidious, and puissant underlying programming that has infected you. (Which is another way to say discover what drives your self-destructive behavior.)**

Are you a baby boomer? Then you grew up with television shows like *The Beverly Hillbillies*. The entire premise of that sitcom was how haughty, pompous, and ridiculous the rich people like Mr. and Mrs. Drysdale were – and how nice, friendly, and ultimately wiser poor Jed Clampett and his family were. (Of course, in the show, the Clampetts were the equivalent of today's dot-com billionaires. But the memes worked perfectly, because it fed the belief that only poor people were virtuous enough to handle being rich.)

Then there was *Gilligan's Island*. Pretty much the running plot line was the ongoing cultural differences between the good, sensible poor folks like Gilligan, Mary Ann, the Professor and the Skipper, versus the preposterous and outrageous behavior of the wealthy Thurston Howell III and his wife, Lovey. (Foolish rich folks who packed hundreds of thousands of dollars in cash and multiple changes of clothes for what was supposed to be a three-hour cruise.)

Another iconic show of the day was *M.A.S.H.* Once again, we have the good guys, Hawkeye and Trapper John, who were subjected to having a pompous, wealthy companion in the tent, like Charles Emerson Winchester III, who wouldn't drink the homemade hooch and preferred rich-people activities like listening to opera. (Notice how both shows used "the III" after Howell and Winchester to demonstrate how stilted and pretentious wealthy people are. Similar to the dynamic in *Green Acres*, another staple of the era. Protagonist Oliver Wendell Douglas leaves New York with his high-maintenance wife to become a farmer – driving a Lincoln Continental convertible around the farm and performing chores in a three-piece suit.)

From shows like these, we moved to a time when the next big hits were *Dallas* and *Dynasty*. Think of how the astronomically wealthy people in these shows were portrayed. What was the underlying programming to your subconscious mind? In fact, the mind viruses against money and rich people were so powerful in these two series, they both were recast and produced again after the millennium turned.

The underlying dynamic at play here is that the more a TV show, movie, book, etc., panders to the mind viruses you're programmed with – the more you will love it. The meme connects with you on an emotional level, allowing you to feel virtuous because you are poor and victimized.

When you see J.R. Ewing, Bobby Axelrod, or some other uber-wealthy character lying, cheating, and stealing – you tell yourself (subconsciously) that you're happy and proud not to be one of those evil, immoral, and insufferable rich people.

Oh, and don't forget all those songs on your iTunes or Spotify playlist...

*He owns a big estate just south of Savannah
And a high-rise hotel in downtown Atlanta
And half the state of Georgia to his name...
She'd be set for life in his colonial manor
He'd lay the world at her feet on a silver platter
But all I had to offer her was the moon.*

"All I had to offer her was the moon." Oh, for fuck's sake...

If you're a country music fan, you recognize those lyrics from "The Moon Over Georgia," a huge hit by Shenandoah. By now you should understand that it is physiologically impossible for a song with lyrics like that *not* to become a hit. (If you're not a country music fan and the lyrics still seem familiar, that's because that theme is the plot line from 97 percent of all the Rom-Com movies ever made.)

If you want more examples of the programming in music, check out the *Billboard* top-ten songs in every category in every year since the list began. Or, if you want to save time – then, like I said – just check the playlist on your phone. I promise you it is filled with songs containing negative memes. My favorite song growing up was "Share the Land" by The Guess Who. I still love that song. But reflecting back on the lyrics now, I wonder if they were written by Bernie Sanders or Fidel Castro.

Every category of entertainment you enjoy – whether operas, soap operas, music, video games, movies, TV, books, crossword puzzles, or plays – has been infected with negative mind viruses about money and wealth. And it continues to today...

I waited with anticipation for the HBO series *Succession*. It boasted some amazing acting talent with an intriguing trailer, so I added it to my TiVo lineup. I watched two and a half episodes, switched it off, and canceled the recording. The show contains so much negative programming, I didn't want my subconscious mind to be exposed to another minute of it. But I knew then that it would become a strong hit for the network. Because the entire focus of every episode is dedicated to showcasing wealthy people as despicable assholes.

At least with shows like *Dallas* and *Dynasty*, some wealthy people were depicted as good (calling Bobby Ewing). In the episodes of *Succession* I watched, there was no such nuance. Literally every single wealthy character in the show was presented as a money-grubbing, sell-their-soul, evil, mean-spirited, conniving weasel – without the slightest shade of redeeming virtue.

Another telling demonstration of the power of mind viruses to influence culture is to look at which movies become worldwide blockbusters...

I could only chuckle when I read about a Chinese studio that yanked a movie from the theaters in week one because it was a bomb. They reportedly spent $100 million making it, and it took in only $7 million. If they would have sent me the script with a check for $5,000, I could have saved them all of that dosh. I don't get this ability by calling Miss Cleo on the astral plane. In fact, there's nothing psychic about it. To determine if a book, TV show, or movie is going to be a breakout hit, all you need to know is whether or not it panders to a majority of people's limiting beliefs (memes). If the script has an underlying plot line where rich people are acting foolishly or immorally – or a greedy conglomerate is threatening the safety of the world to squeeze out extra profits – you're guaranteed a box office bonanza.

There was much worry in the Asian community when the film *Crazy Rich Asians* was about to come out. Because it was the first big-budget, big-studio American film with a completely Asian cast, people were concerned that it would flop and continue perpetuating the Hollywood mindset (meme) that a minority cast can't produce a strong box office opening. But that worry was completely unwarranted. It's just *The Beverly Hillbillies* with soy sauce, certain to be a crowd pleaser. (Of course, it didn't hurt that it stars Michelle Yeoh, one of the most badass actresses in film today.)

The underlying mind viruses in pop culture entertainment are so predictable, so formulaic, that once you discover the patterns, it ruins your enjoyment forever. (If you want a deep dive, read the *Save the Cat!* book series by Blake Snyder. Just be warned you'll know the spoiler of every plot you are ever exposed to in the first five minutes.) Doubt me?

Do you realize that Ridley Scott's sci-fi masterpiece *Alien* and Spielberg's thrillers *Jaws* and *Jurassic Park* – three record-setting worldwide blockbusters by two brilliant directors – are all actually the same goddamn movie?

The plot of all three films is the same timeless trope: a monster goes on a rampage, tries to kill everyone in an enclosed community, and lots of innocent people will die – because somewhere behind the scenes, there are evil, greedy rich people who will make money from the tragedy. If you take the screenplays and swap out the characters, the three scripts are completely interchangeable.

In *Alien*, there is the avaricious corporation that wanted to bring the monster back to earth for profit. In *Jaws* we had the authorities who didn't want to close the beach and lose all that summer tourism revenue. Then in *Jurassic Park,* we have another immoral bioengineering company that would rather let the dinosaurs eat people than lose the theme park revenues. (This will also be the plot line for the blockbuster movie *Covid-19 Pandemic,* coming in time for Christmas 2026.)

The underlying meme of all three flicks is that innocent poor people die because duplicitous rich people want to get richer. (Fun but related fact: *Alien* is set on a spaceship named *The Nostromo*. Director Ridley Scott chose that name as an homage to Joseph Conrad's 1904 novel of the same name. A novel about...greed.)

If you write a screenplay about a scary monster eating people, you'll probably get a profitable teen horror flick. *But if you can weave in a subplot that the only reason people are dying is because there is a rich person or corporation profiting off the carnage* – now you've got box office gold. (If you want to become a successful, sought-after screenwriter, follow that formula, and every movie studio in Hollywood, Bollywood, and Hong Kong will think you have the Midas touch with screenplays. Agents will be crawling naked over broken glass, begging to represent you.)

Note: Here's a good time to sneak in a little nugget about how, in a tangible sense, all these timeless literature themes apply to you, you, you. One of the mantras that every great screenwriter and storyteller knows is:

Stasis = Death

I first learned this from author Steven Pressfield. What makes any story a dud is when things stay the same. From the opening image to the concluding one, something big has to change. There better be a transformation. Because if Bilbo Baggins meets Gandalf and nothing changes, if Jason goes after the Golden Fleece but remains the same, if Luke joins Obi-Wan but doesn't become a Jedi, if the vapid bimbo marries the rich guy – there is no story. The "stasis = death" element is the catalyst moment in every saga where the hero realizes she will "die" if she doesn't change.

Just like our other heroes, you too will have to change. You have to be willing to let the old you die.

Audience members in my seminars gasp when I tell them the movie *Titanic* is the most malevolent film ever made. That movie is a favorite to many, believing they were moved because it's a beautiful love story. They're shocked when I tell them that the more they loved the movie – the more anti-prosperity beliefs they have.

You don't love *Titanic* because it's a love story. You allowed yourself to be emotionally manipulated into believing that. But that is not where the connection really comes from. The emotional connection comes first from another extremely prevalent meme – unrequited love. This is another one of those mind viruses that has been passed down through generations for literally millennia. (And another of those memes in your subconscious that can cause you to self-sabotage your prosperity.)

The unrequited love meme is so powerful because it is fueled by the "I'm not worthy" belief. Being unable to share life with the one you love is the ultimate sacrifice and demonstration of unworthiness. You might be thinking I couldn't possibly be suggesting you may have blown up your relationships or marriage because you are infected with the unrequited love mind virus. But that's quite possible. (More about that later when we get to the "hero's journey" meme.) Some prime examples of the unrequited love meme in literature:

Love Story

Tosca

Wuthering Heights

Don Quixote

The Sun Also Rises

Cyrano de Bergerac

Gone with the Wind

Madame Butterfly

Les Misérables

Romeo and Juliet

The Great Gatsby

And we haven't even touched Éowyn and Aragorn in *The Lord of the Rings,* Laurie and Jo in *Little Women,* Stevens and Miss Kenton in *The Remains of the Day,* Olivia and Orsino in Shakespeare's *Twelfth Night,* poor Quasimodo in *Notre-Dame de Paris,* Jacob and Bella in *The Twilight Saga,* and Severus Snape and Lily Evans-Potter in *Harry Potter.* Not to mention Rey getting only one kiss before losing Kylo Ren/Ben Skywalker to the Force energy. Even the goddamned *Peanuts* comic strip is dripping with this tragic meme. (Charlie Brown loves the Little Red-Haired Girl, Peppermint Patty loves Charlie, Sally loves Linus, but Linus loves his teacher, and Lucy loves Schroeder, who loves...only to play Beethoven.)

But the timeless unrequited love trope is just the tip of the iceberg (snarky pun intended) as to why millions of people adore *Titanic*. The other reason is virtually every scene of the movie, level upon level upon level, is drenched with negative subliminal memes about money and rich people.

The first scene opens with Bohemian vagabond Jack Dawson. Now why is Jack so happy? Because he's broke. A guy like him doesn't have to worry about the Bentley getting a flat, the butler calling in sick, or the high cost of private jet maintenance. He has nothing to lose, just lives in the moment and is rewarded by winning the cruise in a card game. What's the subliminal message? Poor people are happy-go-lucky.

Scene two we meet Rose. Rose is definitely not happy, she's fucking miserable. Why? Because her mom has arranged a marriage for her to Cal Hockley, an abusive and controlling jerk who is an heir to his daddy's steel fortune. What's the subliminal message? You sell your soul for money.

Remember the scene in the first-class dining room? Miserable Rose is trapped with Cal and all of the boring society people at mealtime. There are brandy snifters, cigars, champagne, and people who know how to use that fourth little fork on the left. As the pompous rich people blather on, Rose is picturing her future life of desperation. What's the subliminal message? Rich people are no fun at all.

Then Jack accosts Rose and takes her down to third class, where they know how to party. (Notice it couldn't even be second class. Had to be third.) Down there, people are joyous and jovial, singing and dancing, living life to the fullest. What's the subliminal message? Poor people are a lot of fun to be around.

Then the ship hits an iceberg and what happens next?

The poor people are literally chained up in the bowels of the ship, while the rich people row off into the sunset. Those rich people fight to get into lifeboats, and Cal steals a baby trying to jump the line over a woman. What's the subliminal message? Rich people are despicable, heartless animals.

Fast forward eight decades...

Rose is now 101 and being taken care of by her granddaughter. She still has the invaluable blue diamond that Cal gifted her. She could give it to her hard-working granddaughter and set her up for life, but what does she do? She feeds it to the goddamned sharks. What's the subliminal message? If you're wealthy, you should just go stick your head in an oven.

Level after level after level after level, you are brainwashed with negative mind viruses on money and wealthy people. And that's why *Titanic* became the highest grossing movie since the earth's crust cooled.

At least until Cameron made his next masterpiece, *Avatar*. Which eventually overtook the worldwide revenues of *Titanic*. And what, pray tell, was the plot line of Avatar?

Representatives of a wicked, gluttonous corporation travel to the lush world of Pandora, where they intend to drive off or exterminate the native Na'vi people and plunder the planet's valuable natural resources. Just to make the memes perfect, the protagonist, Jake Sully, is a paraplegic in a wheelchair, and we learn that a spinal injury like his can be fixed with enough money. If he is willing to sell out the Na'vi, the evil corporate overlords will finance an operation so he can walk again. The plot meets the exact formulaic criteria to become a smash pop culture phenomenon. (Which it did.) The monster (in this case the Marines) is killing off the inhabitants, and it's happening in an enclosed community (the world of Pandora), so a greedy corporation can make more money.

Give yourself bonus points if you just realized that *Avatar* is the same exact movie as *Alien, Jaws,* and *Jurassic Park*...

We love stories – whether fairy tales, books, plays, operas, television shows, or blockbuster movies – that allow us to hate rich people. Because doing so gives us an excuse for our own failures and absolves us of personal responsibility.

The second I shut off *Succession* was when the patriarch slapped his grandson. This was the culmination in a plot line about the kid's separated parents fighting over how to raise him because, of course, they were trying to squeeze in parenting between their money-grubbing, back-stabbing, pursuit of wealth at all costs. People love scenes like that because then they can tell themselves, "You can't be both a good parent and successful. You have to choose one. I'm sure glad I'm one of the noble, poor people, because that means I'm a good mommy (daddy)."

We love to see diabolical companies in stories like *Alien, Avatar, Billions,* and *Mr. Robot,* because these template plots feed the mind virus that, to become successful in business, you have to rape, pillage, and plunder the environment, and/or exploit innocent people. Then we can tell ourselves, "That's why my business failed. I wasn't willing to hurt people and sell my soul."

That's why you love to hate rich people...

Making rich people the enemy helps hide all of your insecurities, fears, and low self-esteem. You can tell yourself that your limitations and failures are really badges of honor, demonstrating what a loftier human being you are. The crushing side effect is that you decimate your self-esteem, stop dreaming big, and settle for a life of mediocrity. (And in case you're wondering...yes, you can hate rich people – even if you are one of them. Being wealthy can be catnip for feelings of guilt, unworthiness, and self-hate.)

The Datasphere gives you all the raw material you need to do that and remain a victim your entire life. You probably work furiously to become prosperous on your conscious level but undercut your own efforts because of your subconscious self-sabotage programming.

But we have one more timeless universal meme to explore...

That of the "hero's journey." Another mind virus almost certain to cause you to self-sabotage your health, happiness, and success.

The hero's journey is another archetype that has been with us in storytelling – and self-sabotage – for thousands of years. The basic premise of the hero's journey is an average person (the chosen one) is confronted by an extraordinary challenge. They initially reject taking the challenge, then have their "stasis = death" moment, accept the challenge/journey, find a guide or mentor, and ultimately prevail. We love hero's journey stories because we can project ourselves in the place of the protagonist and view ourselves as the noble, spiritual little guy (or gal) fighting the force of evil.

> *"The fates lead him who will; him who won't they drag."*
>
> **– Joseph Campbell**

And if we want to analyze the redundant and formulaic tropes in hero's journey stories – and how once again, they relate to you, you, you – notice this: Usually at around the midpoint of the story, the hero undergoes a death and rebirth – sometimes literal, sometimes figurative – that forever cements their transformation. You'll find this death and rebirth theme in ancient mythology, Jesus in the New Testament, comic books from the '50s, Puccini operas in the 1800s, bestselling novels in the '70s, and the blockbuster movies of today. Here are some examples in pop culture literature of the hero's journey formula in action:

The Lion King

Batman

Fight Club

Beowulf

Tron

The Chronicles of Narnia

Moses

Finding Nemo

Conan

Homer's *The Odyssey*

Star Trek (The 2009 JJ Abrams movie)

To Kill a Mockingbird

The Matrix

Moby Dick

Iron Man

The Hobbit

Star Wars

Ender's Game

Lord of the Rings

Harry Potter

Jane Eyre

The Hunger Games

Avatar

Huckleberry Finn

Dune

The Wizard of Oz

These are the ones that pop off of the top of my head in a hot minute. There are literally *millions* to choose from. (You get more bonus points if you noticed which stories made both the orphan and the hero's journey lists. If so, you're starting to see how the emotional manipulation of mind viruses really works.)

Now let's explore how your love of hero's journey stories as a child could turn into self-sabotage once you reached adulthood...

Let's suppose, like millions of others, you get infected with the "I'm not worthy" meme. Once you buy in, usually subconsciously, you're doomed to self-sabotage because you don't believe you deserve happiness and success. And if you do start achieving happiness and success, you'll subconsciously feel guilty about it. (This is a huge cause of imposter syndrome.) The root cause of all your behavior from this point forward will be based on your low self-esteem. Put in emotional terms, you feel unworthy and desperately want to feel worthy.

This leads to all kinds of crazy, dysfunctional behavior. One of the craziest things I see happen from this situation is how people subconsciously set out to create a more heroic hero's journey for themselves.

In my coaching program I have worked with people who blew up their marriages, bankrupted successful businesses, or found some other way to snatch defeat from the jaws of victory – because they were subconsciously trying to create a more heroic story in an attempt to assuage their feelings of unworthiness.

You subconsciously believe that if you overcome bankruptcy not just once but twice – or beat cancer four times instead of three – or survive getting fired, your dog dying, a meteorite landing on your car, and the house burning down all in the same week – you're going to finally deserve to be loved and accept yourself. But if you don't eviscerate the negative beliefs causing you to manifest all of that trauma and drama, it will all be for naught.

The Datasphere isn't done in its ability to control your thoughts and direct your life. Because there are forces that use the Datasphere to weaponize your fears against you. Coming up next…

Chapter Four

Alexa and Siri Are Coming for You...

HOPEFULLY, BY NOW you've accepted the reality that entities like the education system, government, organized religion – whether inadvertently or not – have infected you since your formative years with some pretty harmful mind viruses. And the Datasphere has accelerated that process in a manner never seen before in human history. You can certainly be forgiven if you've been unknowingly waging a war between the dreams, goals, and desires you have in your conscious mind, versus the limiting beliefs, fears, and self-sabotage programming in your subconscious mind. Now you have self-awareness of that inner war, which greatly tilts the war in your favor. But it's no time to let up...

Because there are forces who knowingly and deliberately are using the Datasphere to weaponize your fears, doubts, and insecurities against you.

This other dimension of the war for your subconscious mind is not conducted randomly or by happenstance. It's not a case of entities who are brainwashed and parasitized, unwittingly sending out memes to you. These forces know exactly what they're doing and why. These dangerous forces are bent on taking all of those fears, doubts, and insecurities you adopted as a child – and adapting them as weapons against you as an adult. Because you now have potential influence, power, and disposable income.

You have become a high-value target.

To see how this works, we must revisit a couple of our original guilty parties: government and organized religion. Keep in mind that in some cases they are united, as in theocracies, which makes them exponentially more dangerous. Obviously, the Datasphere allows them greater means of propaganda, misinformation, and manipulation. However, it also presents a new threat: one party using the memes of the other one.

As an example, governments have now realized they can harness the Datasphere to use religious memes to manipulate you better. One of the common religious memes is about being the chosen one or chosen people. The governments in Islamic countries frequently used fear of other religions to control their people. The Datasphere gives them ways to do this more effectively than they could in the past. And now even secular governments can exploit your fears.

An example is the politicians in the U.S. and U.K. fueling anti-Muslim and anti-immigrant attacks. In 1963 when Governor George Wallace sought to bar desegregation in schools, he was engaging in a futile objective. In 2020 when President Trump would tweet to his 80 million followers, slurring

Mexicans and suggesting that Muslim congresswomen should go back to where they came from – he was weaponizing hate and fear on a scale the governor couldn't dream of. It pisses people off when I say this, but you have cognitive bias in everything. You are physiologically predisposed to believe and be influenced by false information. And the technology that fuels the Datasphere makes this more likely than any time in history.

Forty years ago, if you were a white supremacist, anti-Semite, or a member of another hate group, you might convene a gathering of 11 people in a basement somewhere, or maybe 300 in a Ramada Inn meeting room. But today, you can instantly reach tens of thousands of other people with the same prejudices in a subReddit or 8kun message board. There are cable TV pundits, bloggers, and YouTubers who can spread misinformation or manipulative messages to millions of people in a matter of minutes.

Part of this is voluntary: You choose to infect yourself with this false or harmful information by your choice in sources of information. But now governments are employing this as a weapon against you. Every major government in the world today has thousands of people in both the military and civil sectors working on media manipulation, misinformation, propaganda, and election interference. Their targets for this are the populations in enemy countries, their allies, and even their own country. Really.

All organisms need certain environmental conditions in place in order to propagate. In a similar sense, both religion and government require a nurturing environment: they need you to need them. If you're feeling lost or alone, weak or sick, broke and desperate – you're the perfect target for manipulation and possible control. And they will use the Datasphere to obtain it.

Unfortunately, there is another army of soldiers working to manipulate, influence, and control you – and they know how to unleash the awesome power of the Datasphere better even than the governments do...

They're called marketers.

As Gary Vaynerchuk famously said, "Marketers fuck up everything." That's just what we do. (Yes, I'm a marketer and include myself in this group.) We ruined radio and television, we ruined Internet search, we ruined email and texting, and now we're ruining podcasts and social media. (And if we can't end the affliction of robocalls, we will have ruined cell phones too.)

You know those cool, wood watches from Jord that I sometimes wear on my YouTube channel? They sent me those for free because I'm an influencer. (Not to mention, a watch whore.)

Those 10,000 followers you have on Twitter? At least 2,500 of them are bots.

That quirky Instagram story where one of your favorite movie stars helps some friends move with his new pickup truck? That truck manufacturer gave him that truck and probably a lot of cheddar to post that video to influence you.

Half of those videos of friendly pranks, dogs adopting kittens, animal rescues, and adorable toddlers you see today are scripted and staged by marketers. What you think are random conversations in podcasts, spontaneous videos, recommended links, catchy background music, or helpful tutorials are bought-and-paid-for, relentlessly researched, vigorously tested and tracked content. This content has been produced for companies by advertising agencies that create campaigns that have been curated by an army of marketers employing computer scientists, copywriters, and psychologists. Marketers hire scientists to strap electrodes on people and monitor their eye movements and brain activity. They use astrophysicists who left their careers researching the cosmos because it pays better to build recommendation algorithms and data models that will predict and prod you what to buy next.

Now they're integrating AI to know what you will do before *you* know what you will do. And we haven't even dipped our toes into synthetic media and Deep Fakes yet. We talked about the memes you're infected with in TV shows, movies, and books. How much more effective will they be in brainwashing you when AI can customize every story to your specific confirmation bias?

Right now:

- ▶ Instacart can data mine your purchase history to know whether you should take a pregnancy test. Before you do.
- ▶ Your electric scooter app can track your ride history to meth dealers, cheap motels, and late-night hookups to send you an upsell offer for condoms.
- ▶ Your smartwatch could alert you of a potential heart attack and save your life. And also know the exact second you are physiologically most susceptible for an offer to pull into a fast-food drive-through.
- ▶ Amazon knows if you're gay, straight, or trans (even if you don't) and enough about your fetishes to send you one of those "Amazon recommends" emails for a particular sex toy.

Of course, none of those marketers will send you offers like these, because:

A. You'd get indignant and furious.

B. They don't want you to know how much they really know about you.

I told you earlier that queso-flavored tortilla chips taste better than squash because they are genetically engineered that way. They're also genetically engineered with just the right amount of yeast and sugar to feed the bad bacteria in your digestive track to create a physical craving for more. (Just like that "diet" soda you drink.)

You probably got suckered into leasing your car instead of owning it and are trading it in and refinancing the amount you're still upside down on. Those nice credit card companies offer a minimum payment plan that – should you follow it – will take you 40 years to pay off. You buy a home and pay $186,511.57 in interest to borrow $200,000.

You've probably heard about identity politics. Merriam-Webster defines the term as "politics in which groups of people having a particular racial, religious, ethnic, social, or cultural identity tend to promote their own specific interests or concerns without regard to the interests or concerns of any larger political group." But the real hot sauce here is how the political parties use this information to manipulate you. Because those campaigns aren't run by political idealists, but marketers. And just like there is identity politics, there is identity marketing.

You are being scored every day of your life. Scored sexually, politically, and financially. You think Alexa and Siri are your friends? They're just sucking up so they can sell you more stuff. The big marketing agencies know more about you than your mother or your spouse does. Really.

And once again, the key battles of the war are fought against children. The reason you drink five sugary sodas a day is because you got addicted to them as a child. Do you think adults were the ones clamoring for all of those sweet flavors for vaping devices? There's a reason you will never see an ad for toothpaste, laundry detergent, or breakfast cereal on FOX News Network. Because the average demographic watching that network is over 60, and those viewers set their buying habits for items like those decades ago. I've bought Zest soap for more than 40 years. Why? Because humans fear change.

There are eight-year-old children who have never tasted a piece of fresh fruit because they moved directly from baby formula to Happy Meals. And if you did offer them an apple, they wouldn't eat it unless you put sugar on it. You can thank marketers for that.

And you can thank marketers if you were foolish enough to buy a dining room set with no payments for three years, overpay $15 for a tasteless brand of vodka, are carrying around an extra 20 pounds, don't own a piece of clothing without a logo on it, and just generally live on 125 percent of what you earn.

You can thank marketers if you feel inferior because your neighbor drives a car with higher status than you do, and you can thank marketers if you bought a car because you think it has a higher status than your neighbor's. Marketers will make you feel inferior, insecure, and neurotic – then sell you hair plugs, breast implants, and nose jobs.

This is nothing new...

In the 1950s, the tobacco companies wanted you to smoke more cigarettes. In the 1850s, P.T. Barnum wanted to sell you tickets to his traveling shows. In the 1750s the industrial revolution was starting, and governments were selling you on the benefits of being an assembly-line worker. We can keep going back until we get to 500 B.C., when Grog was offering a "buy three and get the fourth pelt free" offer on wolfskins. Marketers have always wanted to sell you shit and always tried to manipulate you into believing that you were making your buying decisions with a rational mind. But today they have state-of-the-art technology to do so with devastating efficiency.

Back in Chapter One I told you that we're living in the Matrix. That's not a conspiracy theory, because there's no conspiracy by anyone here. The real Matrix you're in right now wasn't a conscious invention by evil parties to enslave you. It's an unintentional, collateral result of the mass adoption of the Internet and its related technologies. The Internet destroys conventional methods of marketing, selling, and retail we have used for many decades. (Example: The way mobile apps like Uber and Lyft blew up the taxi industry, Zillow, Opendoor and Redfin disrupt the real estate business, and streaming programming shakes up the entertainment industry.) This causes industries to adapt and evolve or contract and become extinct.

The grocery industry operates on low profit margins. So savvy leaders in the space decide to add health food aisles, delis, floral departments, coffee shops, and pharmacies. This takes business away from health food stores, delicatessens, florists, cafés, and drug stores. The health food stores fight back by offering beer and wine, and more mainstream brands. Drug stores fight back by adding huge grocery sections to their stores. Everybody fights the war by adding additional product lines and services. Suddenly even beauty salons are selling jewelry, workout apparel, and diet teas.

Mega retailers like Walmart come on the scene and become the new Death Star, competing by selling a wide variety of products – from groceries to clothing, electronics to tires, movies to home décor, prescription drugs to sporting goods, toys to patio furniture. They want to sell everything every other store sells while eyeing up online retailers. Amazon enters next and becomes the online Death Star, while eyeing up brick-and-mortar stores. As the retailers fight the war against each other, along come delivery services like Instacart, DoorDash, Peapod, and others that change the game again. Walmart answers with in-store delivery and Amazon one-ups them with *Prime*. (Next thing you know, there's a worldwide coronavirus pandemic and everything is blown up all over again. But let's save that for another time...) Similar battles are taking place in entertainment, a multi-trillion-dollar sector. The war for streaming dominance is raging between Netflix, Hulu, Amazon Prime Video, Disney+, Twitch, and Apple.

You probably think these wars are for the territories of retail, e-commerce, and entertainment. But the actual war being waged is the one for controlling your mind. The new warfare is a fusion of surveillance, data collection, algorithms, and the application of AI to use that data for manipulation of your habits, moods, identity, beliefs, and behaviors. (Mainly by marketers, but with government meddling involved as well.)

This is how the Matrix is created…

The Matrix isn't owned by Amazon, Walmart, Apple, Google, Disney, or even government. This Matrix, the real one, was formed organically from the interaction of surveillance, data collection, AI, machine learning, and algorithms, pulsing and flowing with all of the memes circulating in the Datasphere. Technology advances rapidly. Efforts to regulate technology change glacially. And the gap widens more each year. It is what it is. But that doesn't mean you are powerless. You are not.

You still have the power to determine your own destiny. You still have the power to create a radical rebirth for yourself.

Once you recognize this, once you see the Matrix for what it really is, you get to fight back. You can eviscerate the limiting beliefs you've been programmed with and replace them with empowering ones. You get to let go of the old you and create the new, improved version you want.

But if you're serious about doing that, you better get pissed off. You should be furious about all of the people, companies, and institutions that are emotionally manipulating you to do what they want you to do and buy what they want you to buy. And after you're done being furious, you better get focused, determined, and resourceful. You're going to have to get smarter, become a critical thinker, recognize the programming you're receiving and counterprogram against it. And that's what we will look at next…

74 | RANDY GAGE

Chapter Five

Blowing Up Bad Beliefs About Money and Success

HOPEFULLY, BY NOW you realize that the majority of the programming you're receiving daily is designed to keep you ignorant, sick, needy, victimized, lonely, and/or broke. The key to creating a new you – one that you like to hang out with – is identifying the limiting beliefs you created from that programming and replacing them with empowering ones.

Let's revisit the six areas of core, foundational beliefs that determine your self-esteem and the levels of happiness and success you achieve. In each area, we'll explore the direct connection between a negative belief and the results you manifest – and the type of belief you must create to replace the old belief. Here they are again:

- Money/Success
- Marriage/Relationships
- Sex/Sexuality
- God/Religion
- Health/Wellness
- Career/Work

We'll start this chapter with the negative beliefs surrounding money and success. The main memes in this category are:

- ▶ Money is bad.
- ▶ It's noble or spiritual to be poor.
- ▶ You don't deserve success.
- ▶ Rich people are evil.
- ▶ You have to be a bad parent to become successful.
- ▶ Successful companies have to exploit people and the environment.
- ▶ Money and material possessions have nothing to do with happiness.

The main results of these memes are to cause you to hate wealthy people and identify yourself as superior to them – believing that being poor makes you more spiritual, noble, or virtuous. They can also cause you to set your goals lower and self-sabotage your success.

First let's get some of the silly beliefs out of the way...

Let's start with the misconception about money being bad or evil. Money is simply a medium of exchange. Governments attempt to assign it a unilateral worth, but it actually fluctuates all the time. The only real value of money is what you're willing to receive or trade it for. Money is neutral; there is nothing bad about it or good about it

BLOWING UP BAD BELIEFS ABOUT MONEY AND SUCCESS

– unless you knowingly or unknowingly attach an emotion or motive to it.

If you think about this subject rationally, you have to realize there is no connection between money and whether a person is good or evil. Money simply reveals who you really are. If you're a grounded person with positive self-esteem and strong character, coming into a large amount of money would lead you to use it for higher good for yourself and others. If you're a dishonest, narcissistic person who comes into a large amount of money, you'll use it to control and manipulate others for your personal gain.

You'll frequently hear statements like "money doesn't buy happiness," "a car simply gets you from point A to point B," and my favorite, "once you turn the lights off, all hotel rooms are the same." People who make statements like these believe it brands them as wise and virtuous. In actuality, such proclamations expose their ignorance.

We can agree that money doesn't buy happiness. But can we also agree that poverty doesn't buy happiness either? Anyone who has ever driven a Viper or Ferrari, or been ensconced in a Bentley Continental GT, would never be so foolish to suggest there is no difference in the possible methods of transit between the aforementioned points A and B.

Likewise, no rational person would say there is no distinction between an oceanfront suite at the Four Seasons versus a room at the Holiday Inn overlooking the dumpster behind the IHOP. Or at least no rational person who wasn't under the influence of worthiness mind viruses. (And trust me, even in the dark, there's still quite a difference in the air quality, cleanliness, soundproofing, mattress, and bedding.)

Now, if you decide that it is prudent for your financial situation to book a room with a brick-wall view versus one with a panoramic vista, or to stay at the Marriott instead of the Mandarin Oriental, that may be the sensible choice for you. But make those choices rationally, not because of ridiculous misrepresentations. Money and material things don't make you happy, but they do allow you the self-expression, freedom, and enjoyment that can make you happier.

Here are some ways to turn negative beliefs into empowering ones...

Let's start with the belief that rich people are evil. This is just more brainwashing, a natural extension of the "money is evil" trope. Whether you are spiritual or evil, having lots of money will just reveal and amplify whatever you are. Today, I'm able to support the arts, youth sports, wildlife programs, and other worthy causes. I wasn't much help to them when I was broke. And you won't be if you're broke either. Imagine the greater good you can do with more money and success in your life.

Yes, there are plenty of companies that exploit workers or put profits over the environment. (And there always will be.) But there are thousands of companies that have proven this isn't necessary for success. They demonstrate that being a good corporate citizen and taking care of workers can make them more successful. Aren't you grateful there are companies to support the many worthy causes in your community?

It's a similar dynamic with the belief that to become successful, you have to be a terrible parent. My mother was left to raise three children by herself. Certainly no one could have faulted her if she chose to go on welfare. But instead, she chose to become an Avon lady and went door to door so she could earn enough money to support us. We had to make our own breakfasts and look after ourselves after school. But what a wonderful example of perseverance, grit, and integrity she set for me and my siblings. You don't do your children any favors by holding back from achieving success or remaining poor. How about adopting the belief that becoming successful could provide a powerful, positive example for your children?

Due to the prevailing mind viruses in the world, you may have coupled money/success with being evil, acting evil, bad parenting, exploitation, or poor environmental stewardship. Once you sever these unjustified couplings, you'll stop self-sabotage tendencies and expand your vision, goals, and dreams. You'll view the world through prosperity consciousness rather than poverty consciousness, and this will transform everything you do. Not only will this make you more prosperous, but through you, the world becomes more prosperous.

Next up, we'll look at the limiting beliefs about marriage and relationships.

Chapter Six

Toxic Relationships Come from Toxic Beliefs

We're digging deeper into your core foundational beliefs about the world around you and how you fit into it. Last chapter we looked at money and success. Now let's explore the beliefs and programming around marriage and relationships.

The memes to watch out for in this category are:

- Unrequited love.
- I'm a noble victim.
- The hero's journey.
- It's spiritual to be miserable.
- Replicating negative patterns from your parents.
- You complete me.

The difference between developing healthy, nurturing relationships instead of toxic, dysfunctional ones creates a massive shift in your mental health, harmony, and overall prosperity. In fact, your relationships could be the most influential determinant, because your connection to those around you – whether they build you up or tear you down, and whether or not they bring you peace, joy, and empathy – will impact every area of your life: health, career, family, and spirituality. (I won't cover all the relationship effects in this chapter, as some are better addressed in the chapters on god/religion or sex/sexuality and will be covered in those.)

First let's deal with the construct of marriage itself. There are a lot of dysfunctional even batshit crazy mandates regarding relationships, especially marriage. Some are religious, others cultural. These include practices and directives like arranged marriages, woman treated as property, child brides, suggesting that marriage is only proper between opposite sexes, paying of dowries, and prohibition of divorce.

The "institution" of marriage, as many are defining it now, isn't really much of an institution. What many would suggest has been the standard definition of marriage since the beginning of civilization is actually a much more recent development. Far too many societies to list have accepted or promoted polygamy for centuries. Some cultures also embraced polyandry – a woman having more than one husband. (For the record, I have no problem with either polygamy or polyandry. I support the right of consenting adults to make their own choices. I only mention them here only to illustrate that all the talk about the sacred and traditional forms of marriage isn't really accurate.) You don't have to like these definitions of marriage, but you can't deny their existence either. For centuries, marriages were determined by the power struggles and alliances between warring families and clans. Some of these cultures make the marriage practices of *Game of Thrones* look mild by comparison. Still today, in a number of places, forced and arranged marriages are the societal norm.

Before you even find someone to marry, the very conventions of it can produce horrific consequences for you in terms of your self-belief and self-esteem. Suppose you are married to an abuser but believe divorce is a sin, are a woman who is treated like chattel, or are a non-heterosexual denied basic human rights. The effect on your prosperity and happiness could be devastating. When we discussed the effects of the Datasphere, I wrote about the unrequited love memes, so won't repeat them here. But it is worth noting how insidious they are, and that they are a direct descendant of the "you're not worthy" memes propagated so frequently by organized religion.

It's definitely worth your time to do some critical thinking on whether you have been self-sabotaging your relationships because you've been programmed to believe you don't deserve happiness in this lifetime.

Likewise, if you've been infected with the "hero's journey" memes, you could subconsciously be blowing up your marriage or relationship (or even close friendships) – seeking to create a more heroic hero's journey to assuage feelings of low self-esteem. Acting out this situation is what I'll call the "noble victim" meme. This isn't just a knee-jerk reaction caused by negative programming. It can also produce an emotional payoff that keeps you in permanent victimhood. Because you're emotionally unable to accept love, you substitute pity and attention in its place. I lived with this noble victim mentality for 30 years. Many people keep it their whole lives.

Jim Rohn liked to say that your income will be the average of the five people you spend the most time with. I believe this principle applies to every area of prosperity. As a result, the satisfaction level of your marriage will likely be the median of the five couples you most interact with. (Or possibly the three couples you most interact with and what was modeled by your parents and your spouse's parents.)

If your parents and in-laws were both examples of healthy, loving, and empowering marriages, great. You've been gifted with some beautiful relationship models. But I doubt you'll be shocked to learn that most marriages today don't fit this definition. And perhaps the most important thing to influence your marriage is the role models you and your spouse grew up watching in your formative years. If one of your parents cheated on the other, was abusive, or they argued all of the time – you probably crystallized a core belief that this is how marriage and romantic relationships normally work. Most people continue the generational pattern of their parents' relationship without even thinking about it.

The other big dynamic that comes into play is how incompatibility of beliefs in the other five core main categories can bleed into and destroy your relationships. Some ways this can manifest...

If one partner has poverty consciousness and the other one has prosperity consciousness, you'll end up fighting over everything from furniture to groceries to vacations to the car you buy. If one partner is indoctrinated with religious beliefs about sex and the other isn't, that's pretty much a blueprint for an unfulfilling sex life. The same with differing beliefs about wellness, work, and of course...religion.

If you're Catholic or Hindu, and your partner is Jewish or Mormon, believe it or not, that's fairly workable, because you both share similar beliefs in the overall concept of marriage. (Though certainly there are still many possible tripwires.) The thorniest scenario is when one partner is not a believer. They often resent making major life decisions based on beliefs they simply don't consider to be true.

I was attending church one Sunday morning with the guy I was dating at the time. There was a gay couple sitting in the row ahead of us who held hands and were lovey-dovey during the service. When we went to brunch afterward, my partner revealed how upset he was with the couple's demonstration of affection. I thought it was beautiful to witness and asked why he was against two people exhibiting their love. He replied that he didn't think it was appropriate to do that in church "in front of the children."

I slapped my forehead because I finally recognized why we were having so many problems in our own relationship. My gay partner was homophobic.

Perhaps you think it's incongruent, irrational, and contradictory for a gay man to be homophobic. Of course it is. But this situation happens often in the LGBTQ community and is a big contributor to dysfunctional relationships, death-wish behaviors, and suicide. In my partner's case, growing up in Mexico, he was raised with the beliefs of Catholicism his entire childhood. He grew into adulthood and accepted his biological nature of homosexuality – but never cleaned out the destructive anti-homosexual mental programming in his subconscious mind.

One of the most destructive memes for relationships is the "you complete me" one. The number of stories, films, and TV shows built around this meme are in the millions. (With *Jerry Maguire* being the textbook example.) The "you complete me" belief is toxic because it's based on the low self-esteem assumption that you aren't a whole person by yourself and require another to be sufficient. If you believe you need someone to complete you, you're not emotionally mature enough to be in a relationship. And if someone tells you that you complete them, hit the ejector seat. Quickly.

Like the other five categories of core beliefs, mind viruses in this category can cause you to create some pretty harmful results. Let's explore a more prosperous way to view marriage and relationships. First, start with a belief that relationships can be wholesome and positive, and it's not normal for them to be toxic and negative. (I realize that in our society today, the toxic negative ones are considered "normal," but that's not what you have to settle for here.) You can love and appreciate yourself enough to allow yourself harmonious relationships that enrich your life. And you are not obligated to remain in a poisonous relationship for any person or institution. Anyone that wants you to remain in a toxic relationship is toxic. They don't have your highest good at heart and should be treated as a threat to your prosperity.

Replace negative beliefs about relationships with the belief that they are built upon attraction, understanding, mutual life goals, and love. Recognize that gender, sexuality, and the conventional beliefs about them are almost irrelevant. Seriously. If you find someone who excites and inspires you, someone who brings joy to your life and you bring joy to theirs, and you want to share your life with them, then do that and stop seeking approval from anyone or any institution. Approval from anyone or anything else is not required. It is your life. Live it with prosperity consciousness.

As with the other five categories, releasing victimhood is necessary...

If you have fallen prey to the hero's journey/noble victim patterns of behavior, you must recognize that you have two distinct choices: remain a victim or become a victor. You only get to choose one. Choose mindfully.

Next up, we'll look at the limiting beliefs about sex and sexuality...

Chapter Seven

Celebrating Sex and Sexuality

WERE SEX, MASTURBATION, and nudity taboo subjects in your home growing up? Did you enter puberty and adolescence completely unprepared for the raging hormones and emotions you had to experience? You were probably a mess of hang-ups and dysfunctional sexual beliefs before you ever had your first sexual experience. Let's explore the limiting beliefs and programming around sex and sexuality – and how you can replace them with empowering ones.

Sex and sexuality are forbidden or emotionally charged subjects in many religions, and as a result, religion has created a lot of negative and erroneous beliefs on these issues. Most of these beliefs are based upon centuries-old myths, stereotypes, and superstitions. It should be no surprise that beliefs about sex and sexuality are charged with fierce emotion. Making them worse is the widespread level of scientific illiteracy on the subject. The memes and beliefs to be wary of in this category are:

▶ Sex is dirty.

- Pleasure is the road to damnation.
- Women are inferior.
- Gender is binary.
- Non-heterosexuality is aberrant.
- Non-heterosexuality is immoral.

Sexual energy is a primal instinct and one of the most powerful drivers of behavior in all animals. If you have ever seen horse breeding or certain other species mating in the wild, you know how ferocious this energy can be. The human animal likes to think we are more sophisticated and civilized, not driven by these base urges, but while we subdue them, we unquestionably don't eliminate them. Once you understand that sexual urges and energy are a genetic reality, you recognize how foolish and futile any attempt to deny them will end up.

This doesn't mean we must rut in the field like wild animals. As an enlightened species, we can and should maintain certain standards for our behavior and must ensure that mutual respect and consent are always present. We should also protect the vulnerable from predators who would harm them.

I believe Napoleon Hill was on to something when he discussed sexual energy in *Think & Grow Rich!* One of his observations was that most men (in a time of rampant misogyny) didn't reach success until their '50s, when they were better able to channel their sexual energy. But respecting and channeling sexual energy does not mean denying it, attempting to repress it, or assigning negative values and emotions to it. Sex is natural and good, not immoral or evil. Unfortunately, there is a tsunami of programming (often from organized religion, but sometimes other sources) decreeing that sex is dirty or sinful. Like so many of the other memes, this brainwashing on sex and sexuality is based on fear, ignorance, and superstitions, with little space left for science and facts.

The Puritans believed that sex led to damnation, but we can certainly operate at a higher level of critical thinking than that today. After all, if it weren't for sex, we wouldn't be here. (The entire Puritanical philosophy is based on the premise that pretty much any pleasure leads to damnation. This is part of the whole crazy "you are meant to suffer here and get your reward in the afterlife" meme much of organized religion loves to infect you with.)

Next, we need to have a discussion about the way women are viewed and treated in the world today. There are still many societies that treat women as chattel, believe they should be denied basic rights such as voting or owning property, and even be killed for wanting to receive an education. You can't have a healthy attitude about sex or sexuality until beliefs like these are recognized as malevolent, immoral, and anti-humanity.

Another contributing factor for many of the negative beliefs about sex and sexuality is widespread scientific illiteracy. Although you may have a hard time believing it, your doctor, the teachers you had, and the people who pass laws in your country all probably fall into this group of people who are ignorant about some basic scientific facts. Let's look at two important ones:

The first erroneous belief is that there are only two genders. This is not even close to being true. You probably have the same basic understanding of gender and sexuality as most other people. For at least a couple thousand years, most people have been taught that when the sperm reaches the egg, the result is either an XX chromosome (which produces a girl) or an XY chromosome (which produces a boy). Although this is a very simplistic explanation, it does happen fairly frequently. But there are a number of other scenarios that also play out quite commonly. In fact, there are almost 20 known types of sex variations in addition to what we call male and female. Just to give you an idea, here are a few of them.

Ullrich-Turner Syndrome manifests as several conditions in females, where all or part of the sex chromosomes are absent. Characteristics can range from small stature or a low hairline to nonworking ovaries and sterility.

With *Klinefelter Syndrome,* a male has one or more extra X chromosomes, so they could be XXY, XXXY, etc. Most of the time the symptoms are undetectable or could be minor, like hypogonadism. Other symptoms are more severe, such as sterility. These individuals may have a penis and testes, but also show wide hips like a female and have small breasts. And in *Ovotestes* the person has both ovarian and testicular tissues.

Other times an intersex person may exhibit no outward signs at birth, and they don't develop until puberty or adulthood. (Or isn't major enough to become noticeable at all.) That's because genitalia are not the only factor in intersex conditions. They are also created by chromosomes, hormones, and internal reproductive organs. For many of these people, their gender does not match the one they were assigned at birth. The reality is that one in every 150 people is intersex, so the world is filled with *many* intersex people. You could be intersex yourself and not even know it.

Complicating the matter is that, in many cases, non-consensual genital surgery is performed on infants. Many intersex people are born with ambiguous genitalia – a clitoris that is deemed too large or a penis considered too small. Doctors may surgically assign an infant as female, because they assume it is easier to go through life with a vagina than a small or partially developed penis. In the United States, 45 babies with intersex conditions receive this type of surgery every day, which often results in incorrect gender assignment. These are some of the reasons we have people who are born in one physical gender but psychologically are another. While the Adam and Eve tale and other binary gender stories are prevalent, they don't have any basis in fact.

A complete falsehood like binary gender can be accepted as truth because of the tyranny of the majority dynamic that occurs so frequently in society. Certainly, a majority of people are genetically XX or XY chromosome-wise, but that doesn't erase the huge number of people who are not. And they are human too. (Last time I checked, there were 58 gender options for Facebook users.) If you're like most people, you've lived your entire life with binary gender as one of your foundational beliefs about sex. Can you see how this might cause you some confusion in your relationships? And think of all the people who don't fit into the two conventional categories. If everyone around you is trying to assign an incorrect gender to you, you're going to have a difficult time finding healthy relationships and living a prosperous life.

The second area of widespread scientific ignorance is the issue of sexuality or sexual orientation. The conventional argument you hear frequently maintains that heterosexuality is the only natural and moral sexual orientation. The people who make this argument erroneously believe that bisexuality, homosexuality, pansexuality, and other sexualities are a lifestyle choice or preference. But sexuality is not a predilection but a result of genetics, biology, and the evolutionary process.

Because of the various chromosomal, hormonal, and genital combinations nature has blessed us with, there are a lot of naturally occurring attractions in addition to male and female. And it has always been so, since the inception of humankind. From the warrior-monks of Mount Hiei to ancient China, it was fairly common for kings, emperors, and wealthy merchants to have male "pets" or concubines. It was not uncommon for fierce warriors of many tribes

Celebrating Sex and Sexuality

to have a wife and family at home they fought for, as well as a young male concubine. Homosexuality and bisexuality were celebrated in the Roman Empire. (Yes, I'm aware the Roman Empire fell. Lots of homophobic empires did as well.)

You may believe that non-heterosexuality is immoral or unnatural, but that is an opinion you were programmed with, not a fact supported by any science. All sexualities are a naturally occurring dynamic in nature. Otherwise non-heterosexual humans and animals would have been eliminated in the course of biological evolution. There is overwhelming evidence of homosexuality and bisexuality in the animal kingdom, documented in at least 1,500 species. And as far as we can tell, these conditions occur naturally, not because a kangaroo was exposed to an episode of *Modern Family* or converted by whatever the kangaroo equivalent of a scoutmaster is.

The people we allow to influence us the most – religious leaders, government officials, and cultural icons – have seriously let us down. And most of them did this unintentionally, because they're unaware of their scientific illiteracy. You may be programmed with beliefs or persecuted by laws that support discriminating against, persecuting, or even attacking people because of their sex or sexuality. But to do so is against the most basic tenants of prosperity. The resulting fear and ignorance about these subjects are causing people to attack, demonize, and even kill others. But perhaps just as dangerous is the programming non-heterosexuals and non-binary gender people are receiving from themselves.

There is much hate, prejudice, and fear just within the LGBTQ community itself. (The amount of LGBTQ people who are homophobic and transphobic is shocking.) This leads to yet more discrimination, persecution, and abuse. This also plays a large role in self-destructive behavior, depression and other mental illnesses, and suicide. It's simply a reflection of the subconscious and insidious self-hate that memes like these can create.

Let's look at some ways to reframe the discussion and develop healthy, empowering, and prosperous beliefs about sex and sexuality.

Start with losing all negative judgments that may have become ingrained in your subconscious mind. Bring them up to the surface and replace them, just as you would exchange an old coat that no longer fits you.

As you now know, there are males, females, males inhabiting female bodies, females inhabiting male bodies, intersex, and non-binary people who don't identify with any of the conventional labels. We are all equal, all normal, and all humans who deserve respect, acceptance, and human rights. There is no need to fear or judge those different from you. View them with a respectful state of curiosity, similar to what you might experience if you meet an Eskimo, Buddhist monk, or snake charmer for the first time.

Celebrating Sex and Sexuality

If you have questions about your gender, relax and enjoy the discovery process. There are more resources available to you today than ever before. Also, very importantly, please forgive your parents, medical providers, or others who may have made your original gender determination. They were doing the best they could in the environment and ignorance that existed at that time and may have been unaware of your actual situation.

Likewise, if you suspect you might be homosexual, bisexual, pansexual, trans, or asexual – allow yourself time and permission for exploration and discovery. (Engaging a mental health professional can be quite helpful here.) If you find that you are a different sexuality than you originally believed, celebrate and embrace that reality. You have an exciting life about to unfold for you. Eviscerate any negative beliefs you may have been programmed with and recognize your natural sexuality without guilt, remorse, or apology. Love and accept yourself for the beautiful being you are.

If other people have issues with who you really are, that problem is with them. For those close friends or family members who have difficulty accepting you, love them and allow them to grow. They were brainwashed with all of the overpowering mind viruses they are directing against you and may not have the sophistication and intellectual ability to overcome them yet. Give them time. They probably don't read my books! Ultimately, the people who truly love and want the best for you will accept you exactly as you are.

You can't live a prosperous life until you are living your truth.

Likewise, if you and your partner agree on an open relationship, great. If the two of you want to become swingers, play with a third, or hire a sex worker, go for it. If you like pornography, bondage, cross-dressing, role playing, or some other fetish practice, more power to you. Treat yourself to an exquisite masturbation session now and then. There is certainly no reason to deny or repress your sexual desires because of some religious dogma, doctrines, or decrees. Think about the pedophilia and sexual abuse the clergy has practiced for centuries. (Not just the Vatican and Christianity, but within many faiths.) Taking advice about sex from the religious establishment…is like asking for vegan diet tips from Hannibal Lecter.

There is a very broad spectrum of this species we call humans. And *every* member of the species deserves basic human rights, dignity, and the freedom to be themselves. They deserve to fall in love with, be in relationship with, and marry anyone they mutually choose. You have the right to hold different opinions of sex, sexuality, and religion. But any beliefs you have that would demonize, discriminate, or otherwise diminish another human being are anti-humanity and thus anti-prosperity. Any rational critical thinker would understand those beliefs are based upon centuries-old fears, superstitions, and phobias – and have no place in an enlightened and prosperous society. Hate, intolerance, and judgment are not family or spiritual values, and they certainly don't take you closer to prosperity. Leave those beliefs behind.

You can never experience prosperity yourself if you are trying to deny it to others.

Take back control of your thoughts. Focus on a belief that all people of all genders and sexualities can live together in peace and harmony. Here in America, we defined this in our Declaration of Independence as the right to life, liberty, and the pursuit of happiness. No matter where you reside, to live a prosperous life you must support this philosophy of respect for the dignity and human rights of all. To discriminate, persecute, or deny basic human rights to anyone on the basis of their sex or sexual identity is a crime against all humanity. It denies prosperity to both the oppressed and the oppressors. If we want to live in a prosperous world, we must all stand up for each other.

I could write entire books on the batshit crazy beliefs and fears there are around sex, but others have done that already. We've covered enough here to recognize and remake your beliefs on the subject. Now things really get dicey. Because in the next chapter, we're going to dissect many of the crazy, limiting, and harmful beliefs about god and religion.

Chapter Eight

Hope, Dope, and a Very Dead Pope

IT WAS SPRING, 2005, and I was sitting in a coffee shop in Amsterdam, toking up some sinsemilla while the TV on the wall played images of people mourning the death of Pope John Paul II. Maybe it was the dope, but I was profoundly melancholy, thinking that like so many before him, the pope was a very spiritual, caring, and well-meaning human being – who would leave a legacy of poverty, ignorance, and despair for his followers.

If you're a Catholic, or just someone who followed his career, my comments might shock or offend you because you believe the pope was a good person. You might be surprised to learn that I would agree with you. I believe Pope John Paul II was a truly beautiful soul. Yet I also believe he propagated a lot of the most harmful beliefs to watch out for in the God/Religion category. The main beliefs in this category are:

- ▶ It's spiritual to be poor and money is evil.
- ▶ You are not worthy.
- ▶ Women are not equal to men.

- ▶ You are born a sorry sinner.
- ▶ You get the good stuff only after you die.
- ▶ Non-heterosexuals are flawed or evil.
- ▶ Non-believers and apostates don't qualify for human rights.
- ▶ You require a god to discern what is right.

Let's begin with the memes that program you to believe that it is somehow noble, virtuous, or spiritual to be poor.

Pope John Paul II was infected with so many harmful mind viruses, he had no idea of the desolation he was creating. He fought communism in his native Poland and around the globe, but I believe he was still infected with the communist brainwashing that it is virtuous to be poor and wealth is immoral. He came to the U.S. seven times and denounced American materialism each time. In fact, he scorned the effects of capitalism at every opportunity – except when the collection basket was being passed around the Papal Basilica of St. Peter.

Pope John Paul II reached out to other faiths – while never missing a chance to let them know that the one door to salvation was going to be slammed in their face in their moment of truth. He was forceful in his rejection of homosexuality, birth control, divorce, remarrying after divorce, and women or married men in the clergy. And because he appointed 95 percent of the cardinals who chose his successor, his rigid orthodox theological vision has continued to this day.

Even now, another generation of kids in church Sunday schools and private Christian schools are getting infected with self-loathing, guilt, and worthiness issues as Christianity marches on. More gay teens will take their lives, believing they have been forsaken by their god. More women will receive the message that they are second-class citizens. More people will stay in joyless marriages they never should have been in, living their entire lives in dismal resignation.

When it comes to spreading negative mind viruses about wealth, Christianity is a frequent contributor, but the same type of adverse programming is happening in many temples, mosques, and synagogues around the world. These memes have subconsciously infected billions of people. Think of the many ways this is demonstrated in all of the Datasphere-driven stories, shows, and movies that we discussed earlier. Notice how this programming has infiltrated your everyday language. Have you ever said someone was "poor as a church mouse" or someone else was "filthy rich?" "Mo' Money, Mo' Problems" makes for a catchy rap song, but I faced a lot more problems when I was broke than I do being wealthy. Worrying about how to keep the food in the refrigerator from spoiling because my power got turned off distressed me a lot more than deciding which car to drive today.

If you are able to unplug from the dogma and think rationally, you instantly recognize how utterly senseless and damaging beliefs like these can be. Poverty causes people to lie, cheat, steal, and even kill. There is nothing inherently spiritual about it. And what would be the argument that being poor is somehow virtuous or noble? There is no rationale or logic in such a premise.

Let's venture into the "you were born a sorry sinner," "you are not worthy," and "you only get the good stuff after you die" memes – and why they can be detrimental to the life you want to lead.

Of all the prosperity blocks I encounter in coaching sessions, people's unworthiness issues created by religion are the hardest ones to bust. That's because religion is so emotional for most people, and core religious beliefs are usually hard-wired by the time you are 10 years old. These beliefs can create havoc for you your entire life. As I mentioned in Chapter Two, concepts like original sin, the Eightfold Path, the doctrine of karma, the Jewish Covenant, and the Muslim Code of Law – are all built on the belief that you are inherently flawed and/or needing some type of salvation to be worthy.

In Sunday schools, five-year-old children are being taught that they were born a sorry sinner. In other faiths, youngsters are taught that they may need to live for 150 lifetimes until they reach enlightenment. How are they expected to feel worthy if they are only on lifetime number 97? What about the kids who are taught that they were reincarnated in this lifetime only to pay penance for bad deeds they did in the last one? How do you think that affects their self-esteem?

Up to now, we've been discussing the internal issues religions create about worthiness. But we should also explore the external issues that can manifest. Sometimes, outside factors can subconsciously influence you to believe that you are somehow lesser because of your faith. As I'm writing this, in China more than a million Muslims have been arbitrarily detained in reeducation camps in Xinjiang Province. Most of them are Uighur, a predominantly Turkic-speaking ethnic group. Think of how being persecuted like this could cause self-doubt and affect your self-esteem.

Of course, I would be remiss if I didn't mention the Jews and what they have faced as a people. On the conscious level, they are taught to have belief in their faith. Start with the belief that they are the chosen people, how Jewish values like the Ten Commandments and the Torah stand at the foundation of American values, and their pride about the accomplishments of so many of the Tribe. (Jews have about 30% of all scientific Nobel Prizes while only 0.2% of the population, etc.)

But what about on the subconscious level?

Christians speak of the Judeo-Christian tradition, but many have mixed feelings, fears, and sometimes a hate of Jews. (It's why there are courses on Judeophobia in Hebrew universities.) Christians have received very conflicting messages. First that they are supposed to honor Jews (Genesis 12:3), while at the same time Jews are referred to as the spawn of Satan in John 8:44. And since a major precept of Christianity is that you can only get a ticket to heaven by accepting Jesus as your savior, that opportunity excludes Jews, as they are commanded to love only god. To any indignant Christians reading this who are thinking, *"How can he suggest I fear or look down on Jews? My whole religion is based upon worshiping a Jew. That would be crazy."* Yeah, that's kinda my point.

Here in the West, you never see lists circulating of Hindus in the media, Sikhs in banking, or Mormons who control Hollywood. But those kinds of lists of Jews are compiled all the time. It's a pretty safe bet many Jews are reading this book, nodding their heads in agreement, but would never entertain the idea to post a review on Amazon or another public site. Why? Because they've been conditioned by their parents and grandparents to keep their head down and avoid the topic of religion in public, so as to not become a target. Even people who are atheist or agnostic, but culturally Jewish, have to be concerned about attack.

And we haven't even touched on the serious stuff...

If your homeland is surrounded by other countries dedicated to its destruction, if six million of your people died in an attempted extermination of your race, you can be forgiven (no pun intended) for developing some issues around worthiness. I don't point this out to edify Uighurs or Jews over other religions. In my mind they're no different than the Hindus, Catholics, Scientologists, and other religions in most respects. But can you see how the attacks and persecution of these faiths might cause them to have subconscious worthiness issues?

Organized religion frequently pairs the "not worthy" programming with the very destructive meme asserting that you are meant to suffer here so as to earn or qualify for your rewards in the afterlife. There are literally billions of people who believe that because they're broke, being exploited, or otherwise suffering – this makes them godlier and thus a better candidate for heaven or salvation. Think about just how limiting a belief like that in your subconscious mind can be, and the self-sabotage behavior it might cause. Whether you believe you're flawed and needing redemption, or you're convinced you're not supposed to be prosperous and happy in this lifetime, or both – this kind of thinking frequently leads to a life of lack and limitation.

The state of your self-esteem as you enter adulthood cannot be emphasized enough. If you have a negative, low self-esteem, this will impact everything you do for the rest of your life. This stage of life is a tipping point for many people, a time when they are making monumental decisions such as selecting a college, getting married, and beginning a career. If your self-esteem is low, you'll make these decisions with lowered expectations, unexceptional goals, and a neutral or even negative vision for your life. From there it progresses to self-sabotage behavior in your health, relationships, and career.

In the previous chapter we discussed some of the hurtful beliefs organized religion spreads about sex and sexuality. Think of the worthiness issues this can cause. Many LGBTQ people are unknowingly homophobic or transphobic. They suffer from unresolved guilt and worthiness issues that lead to subconscious self-hate – which can progress to self-destructive behaviors like unsafe sex, crystal meth and other drug addictions, or even suicide.

This brings us to the hate and violence certain religions practice against other ones...

The Bible, Koran, and other holy books include some wonderful parables that are great lessons on living a prosperous life. They also teach some very dangerous ideas about penalties for apostasy and nonbelievers ranging from imprisonment to death. This begs the question of whether any religion that proposes locking up or killing nonbelievers and people from other faiths would lead anyone to a life of peace and prosperity. What kind of subconscious programming is that creating?

Finally, we should examine the common belief that religion is needed to guide us to what is moral and right.

Joining a religious group seems easy, because you aren't required to do all that messy, demanding, and time-consuming work on ethics, values, and principles yourself. Because most religions (even most gangs and other cults) come with a "starter kit" of acceptable beliefs, philosophy, and behavior. Frequently, when discussing this subject, religious people say to me something along the lines of "I follow my holy book to guide me as to what is right and wrong. If I would be tempted to rape or kill another, the scriptures direct me to a right course of action."

But do you really need a holy book to tell you that things like rape and murder are wrong? Couldn't you spend two minutes in thought and come to the same conclusion? I believe this is a case of people not willing to take responsibility for their own actions and morality and trying to outsource that task to another entity. Imagine if they were to wean themselves off their addiction and take responsibility for living a moral, just, and prosperous life. Which leads us to the most important part of this discussion...

How can you rid yourself of all these detrimental beliefs about god and religion…and reprogram yourself with empowering beliefs about your faith?

Instead of buying into limiting beliefs like original sin, why not empower yourself with a belief in original blessing?

Many in Christianity are propagating the meme that your real life doesn't begin until the afterlife. But Jesus said be of good cheer because he had come to give you abundant life. Consider adopting a belief that your god created us in his/her/its image so we can practice self-determination and evolve into the highest possible versions of who we could become. And because this is a benevolent god, he/she/it wouldn't want us to be mindless drones following doctrines and dogma, but free-thinking entities with the ability to learn and grow – and create our own destiny.

Keep reminding yourself that it is not holy to be broke nor spiritual to be victimized. Being a victim is being a victim. You can't manifest prosperity – or true spirituality – until and unless you are willing to release being a victim.

Make your choices based on values. Any belief system that teaches you are not worthy, are born a sorry sinner, or need redemption from a higher authority is anti-prosperity and thus malicious. Any organization that attempts to suppress your free thinking, or mandate what you *do* think is dangerous. Any philosophy that says you should injure, enslave, or kill others because of their gender, race, religion, or non-religion is evil.

Here are a few questions to inspire some critical thinking:

- ▶ What are your beliefs about god and religion?
- ▶ Did you come to those beliefs by reasoned thinking or were they programmed into you by others?
- ▶ Did you adopt your religious beliefs as a child? If so, have you done any critical thinking about them since?
- ▶ How have these beliefs affected your life in the important areas of money, sex, health, relationships, and your career?
- ▶ Are your beliefs about god and religion serving you or sabotaging you?

All these religious beliefs affect your mental health. But what about the role of your beliefs concerning physical health and wellness? That's what we will examine next...

Chapter Nine

Could You Do Three Pull-Ups to Save Your Life?

IF EVERYONE ON earth had to do three pull-ups to save their lives tomorrow – it would be an extinction-level event. If that doesn't frighten you, it should. And if you're one of the 97 percent of people who couldn't do those pull-ups – you should be terrified. (And work to remedy this.)

We have developed more knowledge about nutrition, medicine, and wellness than ever before. We've advanced greatly in the areas of drugs, medical treatments, and life extension. Yet obesity, heart attacks, strokes, diabetes, and other degenerative diseases are reaching epidemic and pandemic levels. We are the most overfed but malnourished society in human history. For the first time in that history, you are more likely to die from obesity than starvation.

We are digging our graves with our teeth.

This category on health and wellness is the most important of the six belief categories. Even with the massive volume of anti-wealth memes and the pervasive and suffocating beliefs in the other areas – I believe memes and misconceptions about health impact you the most. Because health is the foundational basis of your entire experience as a human being. No one is ever too *busy* to work on their body and mind, only too *foolish* to work on their body and mind. In my case, low energy and poor health were the biggest obstacles I faced to making myself over. I would wager that for a lot of you, it's also the biggest threat to building a new you. This begs the question:

Why would people work against feeling energetic, enjoying good health, and living longer?

Like the other categories we've discussed, this harmful behavior is caused by manipulation of your subconscious mind by external forces. In this case, the primary source of the programming leads us back to our old friends from Chapter Four: marketers.

The main memes in this category are:

- ▶ Food is produced in factories.
- ▶ Good taste equals healthy food.
- ▶ Refined sugar is natural and healthy.
- ▶ Diet sodas help you lose weight.
- ▶ Bread is the staff of life.
- ▶ Prescription drugs negate poor life choices.
- ▶ Daily exercise is only for professional athletes.

Note: I'm not a nutritionist or dietician and have no desire to be the food police. I'm not going to get into the weeds here in terms of specific diets, exercise routines, or medical treatment. You're not going to find double-blind, medical research studies and statistics. We're going to stay in the realms of big-picture issues and common sense. The focus here isn't to acquire a Ph.D. in health, but to understand how you can protect yourself from daily habits that are harmful and dangerous. Please find a doctor who understands health, not just disease, and consult with other wellness professionals. And there are great books completely devoted to healthy eating, wellness, exercise, and preventive medicine.

Let's start with the prevalent belief that food comes from factories. Most people don't consciously think about this. Food should come from the earth, but 90 percent of the items in their kitchen and pantry come from factories, not farms. We were meant to nourish ourselves with fruits, vegetables, and nuts. Vegetarians and meat eaters can argue about the other proteins. I'll stay out of that debate, other than to say I believe within a decade it will no longer be socially acceptable to raise animals for food. The advances in biogenetic engineering will have provided perfectly tasty alternatives from vegetable sources, and even "real" meat will be grown completely cruelty-free in labs from cells.

Yet for most of the world now, the staples of their diet are things like donuts, chips, pizza, sugar-laden sodas, cookies, cakes, candy, and greasy fried food. This counterfeit food has little or no vitamins, minerals, enzymes, protein, antioxidants, and many other essentials our bodies need to regenerate healthy cells. Our bodies cry out for true nourishment, so we eat more. But while those empty calories we're ingesting provide plenty of fat they don't offer much nutrition. Portions are getting bigger, and so are our waistlines.

What about those pantry items I mentioned? They're items like canned goods, breakfast cereals, and pastas – often with an expiration date a couple years into the future. Cheese spread in a can – what do you think the nutritional value of that is?

Think about the items probably in your freezer right now, like cheese tots, pretzel bites, mozzarella sticks, bagel bites, French fries, corn dogs, Hot Pockets, croquettes, battered onion rings, pot stickers, pizza rolls, tater tots – even all those frozen fruits and vegetables. Check the expiration date on some of those. Look at the amount of added sugar. Do you really think they're giving you much more nutritional value than you'd get by eating cardboard? There are people who believe that eating strawberry pop tarts is the same as eating strawberries, apple cobbler is akin to eating apples, and carrot-cake-flavored cheesecake is the same as eating carrots. You probably (I hope) wouldn't eat chocolate chip cookies for breakfast. The marketers know that, so they make chocolate chip muffins or scones instead. You know what happens next. They've programmed you to believe something that tastes good must be wholesome and healthy.

Many people have breakfast from a microwave, lunch at their desk, and dinner passed out a drive-through window. Fast food outlets keep proliferating, and our busy lifestyles force more and more of us to eat on the go. People everywhere are in serious need of proper nutrition. And simply popping some vitamin/mineral supplementation isn't the answer. It's not so much about what you put in your body as it is what your body can get out of it. Numerous studies have shown that many over-the-counter vitamin and mineral supplements often pass through your digestive track without providing you much nutritional value – and sometimes none at all. These pills are often machine-pressed with thousands of pounds of pressure, so your body simply can't assimilate the nutrition from them.

Next, let's deal with the meme that sugar is natural and healthy. True, sugar is natural, but so is arsenic. Most of the sugar you consume today is far from natural, because it's processed and refined. It tastes sweeter and is more addictive, but its nutritional value is diminished. The American Heart Association (AHA) recommends limiting the amount of added sugars you consume. The AHA says, for most American women, that's about six teaspoons of sugar per day. For men, about nine teaspoons. But we're consuming about 32 teaspoons. That's because 80 percent of groceries have added sugar. Research shows that the majority of this excess sugar becomes metabolized into body fat – leading to the long list of debilitating and chronic metabolic diseases so many people are struggling with.

Too much sugar overloads and damages your liver the same as alcohol. It turns off your appetite control system so you eat more and can cause insulin resistance. This produces metabolic dysfunction, leading to a barrage of symptoms including weight gain, abdominal obesity, decreased HDL and increased LDL, elevated blood sugar, raised triglycerides, and high blood pressure. It also increases your uric acid levels – a risk factor for heart and kidney disease. There is fairly convincing and reproducible evidence that too much sugar in the diet is linked to cognitive and brain deficits – including Alzheimer's disease. And a lot of evidence points to sugar substitutes being not much better and possibly worse. They may be likelier to make you get hungry, eat more throughout the day, and develop diabetes.

The brainwashing about sugar and sugar substitutes is among the most harmful things happening to humankind right now. It's arguably doing the most damage through soda, because it harms your body on so many levels. The average person consumes 50 gallons of soda every year. Diet sodas are not helping you lose weight, they're helping you gain disease.

Bread being the staff of life is another dangerous belief. Bread is the staff of death. Not only is enriched white bread sorely lacking in nutritional elements, it also leaches other nutrients out of your body. The less bread there is in your diet, the healthier you will be.

We're at a crossroads where our knowledge and technology are advancing, yet we're doing little to benefit from them. And still marketers continue the deception and confusion...

Could You Do Three Pull-Ups to Save Your Life?

Have you noticed how much advertising for prescriptions there is to consumers? And what's the focus? That these are miracle drugs that can erase all of those horrible lifestyle choices you've made. Instead of improving our diet and health habits, we take more medicine. Right now, there is an astonishing number of people who take at least 10 prescription drugs on a daily basis.

Think back to what we discussed earlier about the Matrix that is created when memes interact with marketing, AI, and algorithms. Here's the cold reality: It is a lot more lucrative to sell you cancer treatments, medical care, and prescriptions than it is to teach you wellness and prevention.

Finally, too many people have bought into the belief that exercise is something you do a few times a week or that exercise is only for athletes. That's just another misconception put out by marketers to sell you magic potions to dream away the pounds. Everyone needs to exercise every day.

You have to fight back and reclaim your health. Because no matter what version of a new you that you decide to create, you're going to need energy, wellness, and mental acuity to get there.

Let's explore some ways you can blow up these limiting beliefs about health and wellness and replace them with beliefs that serve you...

Start by losing the belief that it's normal to add an extra five to 10 pounds for every decade of your life, because that belief will kill you. Lose the idea that it's normal to take more prescriptions than you have fingers. Change your paradigm to prevention and well care, not medicine and sick care.

Millions of people affirm statements like "I just don't have the energy." But physical energy isn't lying around on a shelf waiting to be picked up. You don't find energy, you create it. You create it by the fuel (food and drink) you put into your engine (body and mind).

Stop making diet choices simply on what is convenient or tastes sweet. Make them instead on how they nourish and energize your body and brain. If you want to live longer, eat living food. If you want to die sooner eat dead food. The difference between the two is active, living enzymes. All raw fruits, vegetables, and nuts have living enzymes. The more of these items you include in your diet, the more natural energy your body will produce for you.

Stop looking for hacks and shortcuts. Everyone needs cardiovascular exercise daily and resistance training two or three times a week to maintain good health. As you create the new you, create a new set of priorities and daily habits to include exercise. And don't forget your mind…

The most damaging belief to your health is thinking it's normal to be connected to a screen 24/7, staying hyperalert to an avalanche of news, trends, commentary, snark, and negative programming.

You're being assaulted with stimuli every waking moment and most of it has negative, detrimental effects on you. To get and remain stable, happy, and sane – you've got to disconnect from the grid on a regular basis. Give yourself the gift of some form of meditation to calm your mind and create harmony. Schedule some alone time and some thinking time every week. Create a workout routine for your brain to keep your cognitive skills sharp. You can solve Sudoku, word games, brainteasers, crossword puzzles, and other exercises to stimulate your mental capacity.

Once you reprogram your beliefs about health and wellness, you'll accelerate improvements in all the other areas in your life. Next, we'll look at our final category of beliefs: The ones about career and work.

Chapter Ten

Rejecting False Identities

IMAGINE THIS SCENARIO: You're a young gun, hired by *Hot, Trendy, Innovative Company, Inc.*, a big international firm with a stellar reputation. People who work for this company are revered and respected in the space. You join with your youthful idealism and begin working your way up the corporate ladder. A few years into your career, you stumble across information that the company engaged in some improper financial accounting. Now you're pondering what your proper course of action should be: report the bad behavior and risk career reprisals or forget you saw this and leave the decision for someone else. Do you think your course of action would be influenced if you had a *Hot, Trendy, Innovative Company, Inc.* logo tattooed on your forearm?

I bet it would. Because to get that ink, you'd have to have made your association with that company a huge component of your self-identity – one you would subconsciously seek to protect.

Earlier I told you that every time you assign a label to yourself, you're creating an identity you will feel the need to justify, thereby lowering your intelligence. I would add that when the label you're assigning yourself is your job or title, this is likely a sign of low self-esteem or misplaced priorities.

In the Career/Work category, the main memes and their related beliefs to beware of are:

- ▶ You are defined by your title.
- ▶ Companies become successful only if they pillage the public, destroy the planet, and/or exploit their workers.
- ▶ You have to be a bad parent to have a successful career.

Identifying yourself by your occupation is similar to feeling you need a partner to make yourself whole. Think of the people whose primary identity is as a parent or spouse to a famous person. That's an incomplete, superficial self-identity that rarely ends well. Defining yourself by a title is a very limiting way to view yourself. If you see yourself as an accountant, physician, attorney, etc. – who are you if you lose your license or accreditation for some reason? (Full disclosure: That last sentence was written by someone who fiercely identifies himself as a writer.) Work should be something you do – not who you are.

Let's unpack the second belief, that companies must engage in malevolent behavior to be successful...

As I'm writing this, we're in the process of the next presidential election in the U.S. As is always the case, there's lots of talk about millionaires and billionaires, and you can imagine the type of inferences these conversations contain. Also, lots of talk about companies and how much they pay in taxes. The current target of attack is Amazon, which allegedly earned a $2.5 billion profit and paid zero in taxes. Amazon makes for an easy villain here. But if we look at the issue mindfully, things are a little more complex.

Amazon takes advantage of many tax credits for investing for the future. Many of those tax breaks were created expressly for the purpose of encouraging companies to stay relevant by investing for the future, and Amazon has done that magnificently. The company now provides jobs to one million people. That's a lot of paychecks, providing income to households that *is* taxed, creating a profound ripple effect for the overall economy. It's safe to assume the company pays massive amounts of sales, state, and real estate taxes. To suggest that they are a zero-sum contributor to government coffers isn't a rational argument.

Now, having said that...

Is the U.S. tax code fair? I certainly don't think so. And evidence shows the last tax cut benefited the wealthiest people and companies disproportionally better than lower-income Americans. The disparity is getting worse. Still I didn't send in any extra income tax and I bet you didn't either. So why blame Amazon for taking advantage of every lawful tax break they are entitled to – just as you and I did?

If you want to rewrite the tax code, great. Want to donate more money to charity, great. But don't make Jeff Bezos the villain. That's just falling into the mind viruses about wealthy people being evil. Bezos is doing his job as CEO to provide a return on investment for his investors. (Many of whom stood by and believed in the company in the early years when it was losing millions and millions of dollars.)

We can agree the tax system needs reform without coming to the conclusion that companies must rape, pillage, and plunder in order to be successful. Because the latter belief doesn't serve you. There are many proponents of conscious capitalism who demonstrate that it is possible to become a successful company and still serve your customers, employees, and society in general. You can argue that more companies choose the shortcuts, but that doesn't invalidate the premise.

If you believe that companies have to be bad actors to become successful, you're even more likely to fall into the next limiting belief – that you must choose between your family and a career. (Or that to choose a career requires you to be a bad parent.)

Rather than spend more time than necessary on this, let's keep it simple. There are stay-at-home parents who are mentally or physically abusive to their children, and there are people with successful careers who are model parents. Whether or not you work at a job, or whatever kind of work you do, these are not the defining criteria for being a good parent. The criterion is good parenting.

Now that you are aware of the beliefs you want to avoid or reprogram, let's look at some beliefs that are more empowering for you...

Rejecting False Identities

Not everyone enjoys a job that is considered to be for the greater good (teaching school, nursing, researching a cure for cancer, etc.). If Julio works in a lab studying DNA in an attempt to prevent multiple sclerosis, and Ben works as an attorney, does that make Julio a better person? Not in the least. Because your occupation doesn't determine your value as a human being.

Earning more money will not increase your self-worth either. The way in which you earn money – the actual service and value you create with your work – has a much stronger effect on how you view yourself. Having a more prestigious title won't make you a better person either. Earnings and occupational titles have no more bearing on your attributes as a person than a car's color does to its ability to go faster. Even the cancer researchers need someone to drive the buses, harvest the oranges, and install the streetlights. If you do your work honestly and provide the value you are hired to do, you're contributing to a prosperous equation.

Some people are able to find a career that they are passionate about, helps the greater good, and allows them to become wealthy. Others do work they're passionate about and the financial rewards are not there. Still other people do work that provides tremendous financial reward, but they're not passionate about it. You might choose to be a schoolteacher knowing it doesn't have as high a financial upside as a stockbroker but are at peace with that reality. Or you might choose to be a stockbroker, amass a fortune, and then finance schools in the third world. Recognize that your job, title, or occupation won't determine whether you are an enlightened human being or live a prosperous life.

An empowering belief to live by is that no matter what your job or career is, you can choose a path of enlightenment and prosperity. And you do that by how you actually live your life, the habits you create, and the choices you make on a daily basis.

Here's one more belief I suggest you adopt...

You don't discover your assignment in life. Your assignment discovers you, provided you are mindful enough to notice. And the universe won't provide you with your next assignment until you are overqualified for your current one. If you set the intention to live each day with curiosity and wonder, seek harmony and enlightenment, and commit to growth and learning, you'll find interesting and fulfilling work to match your progress on the journey.

Now that we've broken down the most dangerous beliefs in the six main categories – and found some empowering ones to replace them with – let's explore something that can become an incredible catalyst for your rebirth, and that is *divine discontent...*

Chapter Eleven

Living in Divine Discontent

It was 9:15 am when I pulled up to my pizza joint to prepare for letting in my staff, receiving deliveries, and opening at 11. I noticed two guys lounging by a car parked in front. When I started to turn the key in the door, they approached and introduced themselves. They were agents from the Internal Revenue Service, responding in person to a letter I had sent to the agency requesting a payment plan to pay my delinquent payroll taxes.

They had a very simple payment plan to offer...

Counting the late penalties and interest, my debt was $55,000. Their offer: I write them a check for the total amount on the spot, or they would padlock the door and seize the business. Since the balance in my checking account was at least $54,000 shy of that, they allowed me 15 minutes inside to make some frantic but unsuccessful phone calls and then they put on the padlock.

While the agents were outside, I had emptied the safe and the cash register of the approximately $750 in there to offer my employees as the only severance package I could provide and called the vendors to explain the situation and cancel all deliveries.

The car I drove was leased, the apartment I lived in was rented, and the few credit cards I had were maxed out. I had no savings, no job, and no resources to fall back on. I drove mindlessly to I-95 and headed north, crying in the car, reflecting on the humiliation and shame I would feel trying to explain the situation to my family and friends.

This was my second big entrepreneurial venture and my second big disaster. The first had happened when I was 18 or 19. Sold my furniture, slept on the floor, and ate macaroni and cheese three times a day. Not Kraft, the good stuff, because that cost three boxes for a dollar. I ate the store brand, because I could get four boxes for a dollar. (Obviously, I've just outed myself as a Boomer, because this was many years before it was trendy to be a struggling startup founder eating Ramen noodles.)

Make no mistake: If you have never sold all your furniture and slept on the floor – it sucks. I mean totally sucks. Selling a few lamps and end tables is humiliating, but not all that life-altering. But when it comes down to "go time" on the kitchen table, sofa, and the bed – suck reality hits quickly. If you're like me, the last thing you sell is the TV, because you while away your insomnia watching mindless sitcoms and infomercials of get-rich-quick schemes to try and forget your life of loud desperation.

When you're 18 or 19, there is something surreally romantic about it all. Making your way back, building brick-and-board bookcases, finding someone's old sofa on the curb you can throw a sheet over, fighting the valiant fight. But when you're over 30,

Living in Divine Discontent

your friends are married with kids, houses, jobs, and money – that perverse romanticism fades really quick-like. It pretty much just plays out as all sucky, all the time.

Making it all worse, my business failures were just the beginning of my drama. A series of health challenges and toxic relationships were also culminating at the same time – all creating the perfect storm of a dysfunctional, miserable existence. I wanted to kill myself but didn't have the guts. Fortunately, I then had a better idea: To once again kill the old me and replace it with a new and improved version. Because I realized that I didn't just hate my life – I hated myself. Looking at who I had become, I couldn't stand that guy. He was weak, ignorant, and a professional victim. So, I killed him.

Once you have released the negative beliefs in the six core areas we discussed earlier – and replaced them with empowering beliefs – you are at the perfect state of mind to re-create yourself. Creating a new you is not easy. There are lots of unexpected twists, disappointments, and challenges along the way. But if you don't like the old you and you stay that person – you'll be miserable for the rest of your life.

You will never pay a higher price for anything than you'll pay for living your dream. Except for the price you'll pay if you give up on that dream.

The reason I'm sharing my story is so you can extrapolate my experience onto yours and see your way to creating a new version of you, one that you will love. In my case, I was sick and tired of being sick and tired, so I set out to learn how to be healthy and energized. I hated working 18-hour days in a greasy restaurant and had always dreamed of being a writer. I wrote a story and submitted it cold to the editor at *Miami New Times* and he bought it. I took the General Equivalency test to get a high school diploma so I could audit some college courses. It would be cool to say that everything changed in an instant, but that would be a lie. It took about two years, but at the end of that time, I felt like a totally different person. (Not coincidentally, it takes about two years for your body to totally regenerate all your cells. In two years you literally are a completely new person.)

Next, began the period of transformation from poor to wealthy. This was a process of learning how to build businesses and make money. By learning those skills, I became wealthy. This provided the opportunity to buy exotic sports cars, $10,000 shoes and $65,000 watches, fly the Concorde, collect art, spend $500 a week on fresh flowers, and get regular massages, manicures, pedicures, and facials. (Full disclosure: The rest of the money I just pissed away.)

Those were heady days, filled with success, recognition, and living large. But there was something missing. My calendar was full, but my life was empty. The situation seemed to be an unsolvable mystery. There were four things I was fairly certain of:

Living in Divine Discontent

1. I believed teaching was my destiny. I knew I was meant to write books, teach seminars, etc.
2. I wanted to write and speak more.
3. I *loved* writing and speaking.
4. But at that moment in my life, I was feeling entirely burnt out with absolutely no idea how I could write or speak anything of value to anyone.

Something was seriously out of sync. A guy who was born to teach and loved to teach should never get too burnt out to teach. I set my intention to discover the cause of this contradiction. This led me to unplug from the world and go on a two-year sabbatical. I sold my place and everything in it, left with what fit in my roller-board suitcase, and headed to the airport.

I wasn't sure if I was going to meditate in a mountain cave in Tibet, infiltrate a lesbian commune, or start a boy band. And I didn't care. All that mattered was killing off that person I didn't want to be any longer – and creating the new, improved model I was excited to become. That sabbatical was a time of deep introspection and discovery. Along the way, I solved my ambiguity about burnout. Here's what I discovered:

You don't get burned out because you are giving too much. You get burned out because you are trying to give something you don't possess. You have to give something that is created within you – and when you do that, the supply is infinite.

When you find something that you are truly passionate about, when it springs forth unbidden from your very essence, you can never get burned out with it. Most world class tenors play three or four roles they're famous for and do nothing else. Placido Domingo performs more than 130. Over dinner one evening I asked him if that was because he was seeking a greater challenge. "It's nothing to do with challenge," he told me. "I have passion for the music. And even if I lived three lifetimes, I could never perform all the music I love." At the time, his answer surprised me, but today it makes perfect sense. Music springs forth from the very essence of the maestro; the music is who he is.

My sabbatical was transformational in so many ways. In addition to my epiphany about burnout, I changed my perspective about money and success. I began sifting everything through a filter of meaning. Desire for success gave way to desire for significance. Another rebirth took place.

But transformation into becoming the new you isn't a "one and done" event. It's an ongoing, continuing adventure. It's been just over five years since the sabbatical and since then I have once again murdered an outdated version of me that was no longer serving me. (What my close friends, as they glance knowingly at each other, describe as "Randy's fourth mid-life crisis.")

You might think I'm desperately hoping this version I've created now is finally...the one. Actually, quite the opposite. I'm hoping to hang around on this planet (or possibly another one) long enough to kill off at least another five or six versions of myself. At any point on the trip, I want to be able to look back and marvel at how ignorant I was three months ago.

Hopefully, you feel much the same way...

My fervent desire is that you see life as a series of journeys, shedding old identities, morphing into new ones, and developing your prosperity consciousness to the state I'll call *Divine Discontent*. This state of mind is a spiritual experience, one in which you can live in gratitude for what you have, yet still have an innate hunger to become more.

You create a bolder vision and bigger dreams. These act as a magnet, pulling you to grow more to achieve them. You discover that your level of thinking to that point won't get you to where you want to go, so you develop new thought processes. This leads to a perpetual cycle of improvement, a continuous quest to evolve into the highest possible version of yourself. That's where the breakthroughs live.

It's the ultimate demonstration of the vacuum law of prosperity. You create a vacuum, then work as a co-creator with the universe to fill that vacuum with good.

This all starts by rebooting your system and making sure you're not harboring any bugs from the old software. That's what we will explore next...

Chapter Twelve

Rebooting Your Operating System

Okay, now you're willing to release the old version of you and step into the next chapter of your life. To make a clean break from limiting behaviors of the past, you're going to need to update your operating software and reboot the system. We want to make sure the "new you" isn't being built on any of the old, negative programming. For you to successfully reboot requires three actions. Let's unpack these three big-picture actions first, then we'll explore some of the specific ways to change the programming you're receiving.

1) Implement Learning Curriculums

I used to ask people I interviewed for my podcast to share something they had changed their mind about recently. I no longer ask this because the question stopped too many people cold and the point wasn't to embarrass anyone. Remember in Chapter Four when we talked about how marketers never try to change buying habits of people over 40? That's because, by then, most people have become rigidly entrenched in their thinking and behavior. They stop changing their mind.

This is why so many people feel their lives are meaningless by the time they reach middle age. They have stopped learning and instead simply filter all experiences through their confirmation bias to remain consistent with all of their previously reached conclusions.

To re-create a radical rebirth for yourself, you've got to blow up the human tendency toward entrenchment and regain your neuroplasticity. That means developing learning curriculums that challenge you. At 59, I got serious about becoming fluent in Spanish. At 60, I took up French. Now at 61, I want to learn to play the piano. Maybe when I'm 85 I'll take up mechanical engineering. Or tightrope walking.

As they pursue success, most people seek remedial fixes to fill gaps in their skills. I understand this process, as there are some good reasons for doing that. The problem comes when you believe you've effectively dealt with the issue by reaching a certain goal or performance result. A superior approach is creating a learning curriculum. Now you're shifting the focus from accomplishing a specific task to working on who you become. You develop into the person who indeed does achieve the performance goals or accomplishments, but the accomplishment is not a "one of" thing but a step in the transformational development of you.

Here's an example of what the distinction between the two approaches would mean. Instead of pursuing a goal to crush a presentation with the Board of Directors – you would concentrate on becoming a better communicator. Now instead of just achieving a goal, you're truly creating a lifelong change and improving yourself in a meaningful way.

What does a learning agenda look like and how do you implement it? Allow me to share how I have integrated this practice into my life...

I'm all for improving on my faults and weaknesses. But I don't want to do it at the expense of continuing to improve my strengths. Because eight times out of 10, you will get superior results by spending that time and/or effort increasing action in the areas you're already great in. That's not the case in every situation, but most of the time, you will get a better end result than trying to bring all your skills up to balance.

Example: As a writer, I consider a connection with my readers to be the most important part of my work. Because my books are published in 25 languages, I wanted to connect on a deeper level with more of you. I can employ certain strategies, such as having some of my most popular quotes translated on slides, posting some social media updates in foreign languages, and subtitling some of my videos. (I've done all of that with positive results.) But I couldn't stop thinking about the difference it would make if I could speak directly to more people in their native language.

So, as you read above, I created a learning curriculum to become fluent in different languages, beginning with Spanish. To start, I bought a Rosetta Stone course and began lessons. Next I discovered the Duolingo app and switched over to that. Learning a language requires daily practice, so my learning curriculum included doing at least two lessons a day in the app, reading Spanish blogs, and watching Spanish movies and television shows. I went to more places I could practice Spanish and supplemented my workout playlists with Dandy Yankee, Shakira, Marc Anthony, Enrique Iglesias, and Pitbull.

So far, I'm about 90 percent fluent in Spanish. (Full disclosure: I still must frequently implore many Spanish speakers to "Por favor, habla más despacio!") Last year I delivered a keynote speech to 6,000 people in Perú in their native tongue, so they could read my heart. It was magical for all 6,001 of us. Now, not only am I better able to communicate with millions of people, but I've also developed a skill that enriches my life in countless ways. I've used this same process for learning to write better, winning softball championships, becoming proficient in social media, and improving in numerous other areas as I re-create myself again and again.

Suppose your boss told you that you have to address 300 people and you've never given a speech before. You could simply concentrate on the goal of delivering that speech effectively and not messing it up. Nothing wrong with that goal. Or you could create a learning curriculum on how to become a rock star presenter. Your learning curriculum might look something like this:

▶ Join a Toastmasters group.

- Commit to making two formal presentations every month and find a mentor who would agree to critique them.
- Start attending meetings at a local chapter of the National Speakers Association.
- Watch one video of a great speech every week on YouTube and analyze it for lessons you can apply.
- Read one book a month on presentation skills.
- Attend my annual Speaker School.
- Study comedians, magicians, and musicians for platform skills you can apply as a speaker.

As a result, you certainly will achieve your goal, which is to deliver an effective speech as requested by your boss. But you would also be developing a powerful new skill that will help you in your current job, your future jobs, and many other areas of your life.

Let's suppose you find out that what is really preventing you from becoming a better leader or having a more satisfying marriage is a lack of empathy...

You could create an ideal learning curriculum for this by deciding to read one book a month on the subject and finding a couple blogs or YouTube channels devoted to empathy. Then you might really supercharge your learning by adding in some real-life experiences like becoming a coach for your daughter's soccer team and volunteering to feed people at a homeless shelter.

When you construct a learning curriculum in this way, you craft a much more powerful end result. You totally change the dynamic when you embrace this commitment to learning. You stop viewing life as something that happens to you and start seeing it as something you co-create. Structure your life so you are continually learning new skills, collecting more knowledge, and making your brain hurt.

Limiting beliefs, self-sabotage behavior, and low self-esteem are actually the results of a paucity of knowledge. They come from ignorance – not knowing what you don't know. (And shutting down your capacity to learn.) To create the highest possible version of yourself requires a commitment to lifelong learning.

2) Change Your Approach from Seeking Rewards to Creating Value

Your prosperity is out there waiting for you to draw upon it, but you don't get to just download it like a new show on Netflix. Because true prosperity is a value-for-value equation. You "earn" prosperity by creating value for the universe. More specifically, by finding ways to solve problems and add value.

If you earn $500 by killing someone for a mobster, you've essentially stolen that money from the universe, because you didn't add real value to the greater good. It's a one-time, non-recurring transaction that doesn't create continuity toward real value. On the other end of the spectrum, if you earn $500 by planting crops on a farm, you've exchanged value in a way that nurtures and supports the greater good.

This doesn't mean what you choose to do for your job or business has to be an altruistic act. If you provide a great Thai massage and someone is willing to pay you a certain amount for that, you've created a beneficial value-for-value exchange. But if your focus in life is simply about attracting more prosperity to yourself, you'll end up producing the opposite reaction.

Think more along the lines of the Go-Giver philosophy espoused by Bob Burg and John David Mann in their series of books on the topic. Burg states, "Any exchange in which both parties benefit (they are both better off than they were before) increases prosperity not only for the individuals involved, but for society as a whole.

"Unlike an exchange that benefits only one party at the cost of the other (Example: 'If I want a bigger piece of pie I need to take some of yours, thus making your piece smaller'), a value-for-value exchange, benefitting all concerned, says, 'If I want a bigger piece of pie, and you want a bigger piece of pie, let's collaborate and bake a much bigger pie.' By increasing the abundance of others, you've increased your own as well."

The best way to attract prosperity is to circulate prosperity. Allow me the audacity to suggest there is an additional element to Bruce Lee's philosophy to "be like water" – one that is relevant to manifesting prosperity in your life. When water sits in a pool, it becomes cloudy or stagnant and you certainly wouldn't want to drink it. But when water is circulating in a mountain stream or bubbling up from a spring, it's the most refreshing beverage you'll drink all year.

Continuous taking and misery hoarding create lack and recession. And it's unnecessary because all true forms of prosperity are infinite. Money, love, hugs, kindness, etc., are all resources that can be continually replenished. Giving someone a hug doesn't delete one from your inventory; it provides you a reciprocal hug back. When you circulate substance, you break the energy block and keep the river of prosperity flowing freely.

To those of you who fear you will be taken advantage of, simply set boundaries. And you'll find that most acts of generosity produce generous reactions. Simply smiling and greeting the counter agent before you order your hamburger combo, thanking the overwhelmed TSA agent for their patience, sending flowers to someone, or taking a meal to an elderly shut-in are examples of circulating prosperity and sowing seeds that will come back to you in wondrous ways.

Generosity creates more generosity.

When you're on the prowl – whether you're looking for people to sell to, do you a favor, hook up with, or make you more money – you're probably going to telegraph an aura of desperation, neediness, or greediness. That isn't likely to help you manifest much prosperity in your life. When you change your perspective from seeking value to adding value, you'll be shocked at how much abundance you receive in return. The more prosperity you circulate, the more you'll attract back. Surprisingly, it's not an even trade, because you receive exponentially more in return. The world adores generous people. You can't out-give the universe. I know because I tried.

When you adopt a mindset of generosity, something much more important takes place. You're not just changing your mindset; you're changing who you are. You're starting the transformation process to the new you. That brings us to reboot action number...

3) Dare to Dream Again

Pretty much every child begins with an idealized vision of what their life will be. There are not a lot of five-year-old children who dream of working at Walmart, Pizza Hut, or a dental clinic when they grow up. Most children are pretty certain they're going to be a rock star, football player, astronaut, or the prime minister. Even kids who live in abject poverty, under dictatorships, or within refugee camps still hold dreams.

Many years ago, I "adopted" a group of foster kids who were the victims of the worst kinds of abuse the social services system ever encounters. These were kids that couldn't get accepted into most of the normal foster homes. They had been incest victims of their parents, sold into sex trafficking, raped, had watched their parents get murdered (or in one case, witnessed one parent murdering the other), and suffered many other horrific experiences no person, let alone any child should ever have to be subject too. Yet I was astonished at the dreams they still had, and the level of optimism with which they viewed their future. The resilience of children is extraordinary.

But by the time they reach that border crossing to adulthood, the vast majority of kids – whether the situations I just mentioned, or even raised in healthy environments – have dramatically reduced their dreams and sunk to lower levels of self-esteem. And for many young adults, these levels continue to go down, decade by decade. Don't fall victim to this. What you want to do instead is enlarge the size of the window through which you view the world, creating a new perspective, one that inspires you to live each moment in awe, anticipation, and gratitude.

Of the many negative memes about success out there, one of the biggest is the admonishment "Be happy with what you have." No doubt, happiness is a choice. You can choose to be happy whether you earn $13,000 a year, $300,000 a year, or $300 million a year, so there is some truth in that statement. But that doesn't mean you should settle for a life of stagnation.

This is where the Divine Discontent I referenced in Chapter Eleven comes into play. Because the best way to become more is to desire more. I attribute about 75 percent of my growth and success to that primal inherent need that all carbon-based life forms seem to possess – the propensity to live beyond our income. But in my case, when faced with an aspirational choice, instead of throttling down my desires, I try to find ways to increase my ability to earn – looking for new and better ways I can solve problems and add value and thus attract more prosperity my way. You can do the same thing.

To put this in a prosperity context, it's not about going into debt but creating more value to the universe, which increases your income. Your desire for more causes you to become more. That's why goal setting, dream boards, and activity planning are so important to success. Each of those activities causes you to expand that window through which you see the world. Each time the window expands, you're called to move closer to the highest possible version of yourself. That is the joyous path of prosperity, yearning then earning.

Once you've completed these three actions and your internal software is updated and rebooted, you can start the radical rebirth construction process, rebuilding yourself step by step. Let's look at that next...

Chapter Thirteen

Crafting Your Ideal Vision

CRAFTING A NEW version of you is not accomplished by devoting energy to tearing down the past but to building the future. The radical rebirth process is driven by the vision you have for what kind of life you will live. So now that your operating system has been updated and you've rebooted, let's get into the process of crafting a vision for your new life.

It's remarkable how many people believe they don't have a vision. (I've had people tell me just that literally hundreds of times, both at seminars and on social media.) If you polled the next 100 people you met on the street, it's a safe bet a majority of them would tell you that they have no encompassing vision for themselves. They would be wrong. Because everybody has a vision. What many don't understand is that a vision isn't always an optimistic visualization of an idealized future. That's only one possible type of a vision. In reality, there are three possible types of visions you can have for yourself.

- ▶ Neutral
- ▶ Negative
- ▶ Positive

The reason so many people live in lack and limitation is because they reached the transition point to adulthood with low self-esteem and then, knowingly or unknowingly, created a negative or neutral vision for their future. A surprisingly large number of people in the world have a neutral vision. (These are the ones who believe they have no vision.) They don't expect too much out of life, and that's what they manifest – most of their goals are small and pedestrian. Their primary goal is to make it through the week without getting fired so they can binge Netflix all weekend without thinking of their lives of quiet desperation until the alarm goes off on Monday morning. For them, life is just something that happens to you.

A troubling number of people are in the group with a negative vision. They subscribe to the "life's a bitch and then you die" philosophy. They expect bad things to happen in their life so of course they do. People with a negative vision make statements like:

- ▶ I just can't get a break.
- ▶ My student loans are too big to escape.
- ▶ I don't have the right degree to compete.
- ▶ I'm always a day late and a dollar short.
- ▶ If it weren't for bad luck, I'd have no luck at all.
- ▶ All the good men (women) are already taken or gay (straight).

Notice the frequency of the word "I" in those statements above. That's because, believe it or not, holding a negative vision for your life is a narcissistic tendency. People with a negative vision revel in victimhood and never miss an opportunity to regale you with stories of their latest layoff, medical emergency, or horrific traffic accident. Their vision becomes a self-fulfilling prophecy, reinforcing their negative beliefs. If they don't get a strong enough jolt to question their beliefs and mindset, they follow a path spiraling downward to illness, poverty, and misery.

Obviously, you want to be in the positive group. Unfortunately, the membership conventions for this group have sparse attendance these days. People with a positive vision view their lives with optimism, hope, and anticipation. They have goals and dreams and they are proactively working toward achieving them. If you have an optimistic vision, you picture good things happening and want to prepare for them. You probably think of your future in productive ways like taking care of your health, having a savings account, and creating a retirement plan. You create a positive vision from foolish naivete (as I did when I stated at age 15 that I would be a millionaire by the time I was 35) or seasoned experience (as Steph Curry does when he launches a three-pointer and doesn't need to watch it to know it's going in). Either way works, as long as you believe it.

Much as the negative vision people create becomes a self-fulfilling prophecy of doom, the people with a positive vision create a self-fulfilling prophecy of prosperity. Make no mistake. Each of those visions will influence the results the person holding them accomplishes. It's that way, and it works that way all the time, with no exceptions. Please pay close attention to what I say next, because I'm only going to say it five times:

Your current situation in life is the direct result of the vision you have.

Your current situation in life is the direct result of the vision you have.

Your current situation in life is the direct result of the vision you have.

Your current situation in life is the direct result of the vision you have.

Your current situation in life is the direct result of the vision you have.

Please don't allow yourself to live in denial by thinking your life is a random happenstance or that you have a powerful positive vision but are constantly experiencing negative outcomes by some exception to universal laws. Tragedies, accidents, and misfortunes occur to everyone. But endless cycles of those events occur only to people who co-create them with their negative expectations.

This leads us to the nexus of the issue: The way in which you create your vision and how to upgrade it when necessary.

Having reached this far in the book, you should have a pretty solid idea about the cause and effect relationship between programming, daily habits, and the end result (your life). Here's what the process looks like:

- ▶ Your programming causes you to develop core foundational beliefs. (In the six areas we discussed earlier.)
- ▶ Your core foundational beliefs determine what type of vision you have for your life. (Neutral, negative, or positive.)
- ▶ That vision determines your daily habits and actions.
- ▶ Your daily habits and actions create your destiny.

A prosperous life isn't created in a microwave but a crockpot, and the ingredients are your daily habits. Some of the most seemingly mundane habits – your diet, exercise regimen, how much you sleep, self-development time, etc. – are the building blocks of your health, happiness, and prosperity. How you do anything is pretty much how you do everything.

Daily habits are the foundational element of happiness, health, and success. (And probably everything worth striving for.) If you make a habit of exercising consistently and eating and drinking healthily, better health is the result. If you make a habit of treating people with respect, empathy, and caring, better relationships are the result. If you make a habit of daily personal growth and self-development, success is the result.

You don't actually create a prosperous life. You choose the right daily habits and they create a prosperous life.

It sounds simple enough. But we all know that changing daily actions is not always easy – and sometimes extremely difficult. That's because your habits are simply a symptom of your underlying programming. And just as you can use first principles to create a viable business model, you can use them to create a new you. In this case, using first principles means going back to the primary driver of how beliefs are created: the programming that creates your beliefs and thus your vision. We must reverse-engineer the process above but change the initial programming from negative to positive. By choosing better ingredients for the crockpot, you produce a much tastier stew.

Now you have a Prosperity Manifestation Formula:

- ▶ Elevate your programming, and you transform your core beliefs.
- ▶ Transform your core beliefs, and you upgrade your vision.
- ▶ Upgrade your vision, and you improve your daily habits.
- ▶ Improve your daily habits, and you create a radical rebirth.

This formula will allow you to create the ideal vision of what "the new you" is going to look, feel, and act like. This is no time to play safe, but the moment to be seeking challenges at the fringe of

Crafting Your Ideal Vision

your fear. The person you are meant to become doesn't live in your comfort zone. Nor is this the time to act normal. Normal is the last thing you need right now. In today's world, normal equates to living a life of mediocrity and resignation. You've spent enough time here already. It's time to move to a better neighborhood.

And for fuck's sake, please don't try to be realistic. When people are telling you to be "realistic," what they really mean is downsize your dreams to be safe and normal. (See above.) This is the time to be bold, daring, and imaginative. We live in the most exciting time in human history. Our access to knowledge, resources for innovation, and opportunities for personal development are greater than they have ever been before.

For many of you reading this, you will have the opportunity in your lifetime to buy an underwater condo with a view of a coral reef, have a nunchaku duel against Bruce Lee in a virtual reality holosuite, or enjoy a vacation on the moon. For you to choose a monotonous life is an insult to the force that created you. Your desire for a life of adventure is the real you, knocking on your door, challenging the counterfeit you to stride into your destiny. From here on out, there will be no more trying to find yourself but a decisive approach to creating yourself.

You can become whatever type of person you want to be. Why not choose to become a healthy, interesting, fascinating, curious, joyful, sexy, harmonious, wealthy, successful, spiritual, adventurous, friendly, talented, happy one?

Chapter Fourteen

Becoming the Thinker of the Thought

YOUR **RADICAL REBIRTH** must be created twice. You created it for the first time by the vision you formulated. Now it's time to create the new you in the physical realm. You begin by employing your prosperity manifestation formula, starting at the root: the programming you allow yourself to be influenced by.

Hopefully, by now you have given some serious contemplation to the core foundational beliefs you held – eliminating the negative, limiting ones and replacing them with positive, empowering ones. It is vital that you support this process with programming that will continue to strengthen your new beliefs. To set the stage and anchor your new programming, you may want to speak the following affirmation out loud:

I have grown in consciousness and release the old me. I have gained wisdom from my mistakes. I forgive myself and accept my abundance.

You may also want to put this in your journal or on a post-it note on your mirror. This will be your working philosophy from here on out. For the next step in your journey, you have to create a force-field around yourself – and mindfully decide what programming you're going to allow to penetrate that forcefield. This is how you transform a neutral or negative vision into a positive one.

If you're watching five to six hours of TV every night, it's highly unlikely that you're ever going to believe in a positive vision for yourself. Likewise if you're reading the news sites, spending prodigious amounts of time with victim-mentality people, or attending a place of worship that beats you down every week. You need people and media that inspire you to become the highest possible version of yourself. And you need to be exposed to positive programming in the form of uplifting stories, positive reinforcement, and spiritual nourishment. (You may want to start by subscribing to my prosperity podcast.)

Most people experience life like they are riding a roller coaster. Or if they're really fear-based, the ride with the rotating teacups. Either way, to them life is just a ride they are on – a ride with someone else at the controls who decides the scope, scale, safety, and speed of the ride.

You might think your body and circumstances control your thoughts, but it's actually the opposite.

Enlightened, self-actualized people create their lives by the power of thought. If there is a limit to the power of thought, no one has discovered it yet. Unfortunately, few unleash this unlimited power in their lives. For most of us, by the time we have reached our teenage years, we've become conditioned into being victims of circumstance. Things "happen" to us and we react to them. The moment you accept this, you enter the Matrix. You're no longer living your authentic life but are acting out a counterfeit version under outside control. Your environment dominates you and you're probably subjugated by victimhood and fear.

Unfortunately, many stay in this state of consciousness for their entire lives...

They follow the blind impulse of their dominant thoughts, with no critical thinking about where those thoughts come from or how they were exposed to them. Most of their actions and behavior are simply knee-jerk reactions to the stimulus of external things like marketing manipulation, gossip, religious dogma, government misinformation, and people with questionable motives. They are slaves of these thoughts provided by others, obeying the impulse of the moment, concerned only with avoiding pain or seeking immediate gratification.

You are not meant to stay at this stage. Hell, you're not meant to even visit it. You were born to become a catalyst: to love, learn, create, and evolve. You were born to be rich and prosperous. But this requires self-awareness. Take a sip of your green tea (or a snort of Aguardiente Cristal) before you read the next paragraph, because it is going to break down the single most integral element of creating a radical rebirth in your life.

You cannot allow yourself to be provoked or directed by the random thoughts that are bombarding you daily. You must become mindful enough to think about what you think about.

Ultimately, you must become the thinker of the thought.

That is when you start to access the inherent power within your being. The day that happens, get yourself a birthday cake and blow out the candles. Because that's the day you are truly born.

You are now using your mind instead of being *used* by your mind. You have to be able to step back, rise above your thoughts, and be conscious of them. When you become the thinker of the thought you become the architect of your life.

You stop believing in fate, luck, and happenstance and start realizing that you're a co-creator of your life.

When you can think about your thoughts – as opposed to just being run by them – you are on the most important step to higher consciousness. If someone invites you to invest in their new company and you think, "If it was really a good deal all the stock would already be bought up," you will notice what just happened. You can then ask yourself, "Why did I think that? Is the opportunity really already gone – or am I just having a defeatist thought? And if I'm having defeatist thoughts, *why* am I having defeatist thoughts? What is the underlying programming and subsequent beliefs that would cause this?"

This is the single most important level of self-awareness, the awareness of your thoughts.

Until you develop this awareness, you're always subject to manipulation and control by forces

Becoming the Thinker of the Thought

outside yourself. Once you develop this awareness, you have the ability to see yourself – inside and out – and view the experience you're witnessing the way you could if it was happening to someone else.

What you are aware of, you can direct; what you are oblivious to directs you.

If you're angry, you look for the hidden fear causing the anger. You notice you're acting petty or vindictive, so you search for the insecurity that is driving it. You can't help but notice when you're acting out negative behaviors, and you decide that's not the kind of person you desire to be. You also notice your positive behaviors, then determine you want to become the kind of person who acts like that more often.

What we're going for here is to change your thought process. Here are some actions that will help you in that process:

- ▶ Spend daily self-development time. (Create a learning curriculum of positive podcasts, blogs, and books for this.)
- ▶ Invest in things that help you progress (books, seminars, continuing education, etc.), not things to impress other people.
- ▶ Surround yourself with people who challenge you and force you to be a little breathless to keep up.
- ▶ Schedule at least 45 minutes every week simply to think. (Block it off and do it.)

- Challenge yourself to do one thing that scares you every week.

- Every time you uncover a belief or fear that you can't do something, question the premise. Ascertain whether the action is really not possible for you or you just bought into bad programming.

- Choose to live your life without regrets, anger, or jealousy.

- Measure the habits or behaviors you want to improve.

- Do cardiovascular exercise every day.

- Eat and drink to fuel your nutritional needs, not for pleasure and taste alone.

- Nurture your curiosity. The greatest breakthroughs of humankind have primarily come from people who were curious.

- Have some hobbies and varied interests that cause you to explore new and different areas.

- Create new neural pathways by doing sudoku, crossword puzzles, and brain teasers.

- Begin and end every day with a prayer of gratitude. Keep your heart in breathtaking awe at the daily miracles you experience.

You have to thoughtfully select what kind of programming you are exposed to. And when you are randomly subjected to external programming, you must consciously and mindfully choose how to respond to that. I spilled a lot of ink in the earlier chapters about the subliminal messages infecting the books, blogs, TV shows, movies, religious doctrines, and government information, so I won't belabor it here. You have to mindfully analyze all of these sources of influence and program accordingly. This doesn't mean you have to eliminate all pop culture. (But you should probably eliminate most of it.) You can still have guilty pleasures you enjoy, just be consciously aware of the negative programming they provide and counterprogram accordingly. For example, I'm a big fan of the television shows *The Wire, The Sopranos,* and *Billions*. All three of those series have horrific underlying programming. But as a writer myself, I was enamored with the plot twists and brilliant writing. I chose to watch these shows, but for every hour I viewed them, I found myself needing two or three hours of positive programming to negate the effects.

We are all victims of circumstances and our environment at some point or another. To create your true radical rebirth, you must become a "program director" for your mind. This means you're going to need to purposely select as much of the stimuli you receive and be mindful about how you respond to the stimuli you don't volunteer for. Instead of living in victimhood, you will then become a co-creator of your life, becoming the highest possible version of yourself. But there is still one more area on which you're going to need to run a virus scan and update in your operating system. The people in your life. That's what we will explore next...

Chapter Fifteen

Beware of the Soul-Crushers

ONE OF MY dear friends called me for advice on how to handle her mother who was dying of cancer. My counsel was simple: Stay away and let her die.

I suggested she hire a hospice worker to be with her mother, try to provide for some of her other needs, but not visit her. That sounds hurtful, negative, and heartless, but I wasn't being any of those things. That response was the best advice I could provide to help my friend maintain her own mental health.

Aristotle suggested that the goal of life is to maximize your happiness by living virtuously, fulfilling your own potential as a human, and engaging with friends, family, and others in mutually beneficial activities. Unfortunately, that last activity is the tricky part…

The people you associate with play a dramatic and vital role in how you think, the beliefs you develop, and the ultimate choices you make in your life. Your level of wellness, the quality of your relationships, your marriage, and even your happiness will be determined by the people you allow the most interaction with you. Remember what Jim Rohn said about the five people you spend the most time with? Do you share a cubicle for eight hours a day with a negative asshole? One of your five spots is already spoken for. Are you in an abusive or controlling marriage or relationship? Two of your five are taken. Now you're in a difficult position and down to only two options.

The first option is trying to find three friends who are so angelic, saintly, and positive that they can override all of the negativity you're being exposed to in your other two core relationships. Or option two, which is to remove some or all of the exposure you're receiving from the two who are toxic. Which takes us back to my friend and her dying mother...

The friend in question had been the victim of incest by her stepfather. When she repeatedly went to her mother about it, her mother first denied it, then after the evidence became no longer deniable, she suggested her daughter was responsible for bringing it on herself. Then for the next 40+ years, this mother played emotional rackets, mentally abusing her daughter. Literally, I could write chapters on the other negative and dysfunctional abuse this dying woman has heaped on her family but prefer not to revisit all that. The point is, this woman was so toxic and harmful to the people around her, some of them (like my friend) needed to completely remove her from their lives.

This is not about forgiveness. As you'll see in the next chapter, an important component of your prosperity requires you to forgive those who have harmed you. I helped my friend work through that, and she has already forgiven her mom. But I believed that being around her mother was simply too detrimental to my friend's mental health.

The path to enlightenment is a continuous progression of "upgrading" the people in your life. This is also a necessary element of creating a radical rebirth for yourself. You achieve this by judiciously protecting your mindset, including limiting your exposure to negative and/or toxic people.

It's important to understand the distinction between negative and toxic. Some people are simply negative. They're infected with limiting beliefs, so their default setting on most things is skepticism or doubt. These are the people who tell you to "be realistic" or "don't get your hopes up." You need to be aware where the people like this are coming from. They may love you and want the best for you, but they are still subconsciously influencing you in negative ways. If you're mindful of this, it's not that difficult to counterprogram the negativity. But you may find the best approach is to reduce the amount of time you spend with them. Often this happens naturally, as people move away from each other and interests change. Other times you have to proactively and mindfully make this happen. This isn't about being arrogant or thinking you are better than other people. (Although in many cases you might be.) You have to recognize that different people are on different journeys.

Your best bud, who was the drummer of your rock band in high school, may not be going the same direction as you when you guys are 35. Your drinking buddies when you were 20 may not be an empowering influence on you when you are in your forties. Different people grow to different levels of awareness and reach them at varying speeds.

One of the most disappointing things about choosing a path of personal growth and development is that not everyone in your life will also choose this path. You will start to notice that some of the people surrounding you are not keeping up.

- ▶ You want to watch *Nat Geo* and they want to watch *The Bachelor*.
- ▶ You want to play chess and they want to find a happy hour.
- ▶ You desire to live in harmony and they feed off of drama and dysfunction.
- ▶ You like to eat healthily and they like to drug and drink.
- ▶ You set aside money for retirement and they want to bet it on the Lotto.
- ▶ You like to exercise and they like to binge-watch reality shows.

Recognizing this, you realize you need to start lowering your exposure to certain people. Maybe instead of meeting for dinner once a week, you change to every other week or once a month. You may decide to reduce your participation in or exposure to various groups, social events, or environments.

At the same time, you consciously work to find and attract people who are operating at a higher consciousness, who you can bring more into your life. When you become serious about self-development and personal growth – you make this a conscious, mindful process. You don't create criteria of a certain net financial worth, but you do look for people who are manifesting prosperity, harmony, and abundance in their lives. You look to bring them into your life and think about how you can add value to theirs.

At other times, there are people in your life who are undeniably toxic. Toxic people could have serious mental issues, they're determined to be a victim so they "fight dirty," or they are evil and want to abuse, control, or sabotage your happiness and success. One of the most chilling realizations you can come to is recognizing you have someone in your life who is so toxic and/or abusive, you need to completely remove them from your world. But remove them you must. Because your mental health, happiness, or even your life may depend on it. Abusers left unchecked often get progressively more dangerous and violent. And they are experts at manipulating their victims and leading them to believe the abuse is their own fault.

Maybe your religion teaches you that you must stay in a threatening relationship no matter what is happening to you. That's simply cult-level, brainwashing bullshit. Maybe you believe because someone is your blood relative or spouse you must accept whatever they throw at you. That's more craziness. (And they will attempt to use your guilt against you to suppress you further.) No one has the right to emotionally, physically, or sexually abuse you. No one. If you feel physically threatened, you need to seek out the authorities and mental health professionals. There really are situations where it is appropriate, even necessary, for you to completely remove someone (even a family member) from your life forever.

You are born with the inherent birthright of living a life of prosperity. Don't let anyone steal that from you.

Hopefully, you're not facing physical harm or abuse. However, there may be people in your life who don't pose a physical threat, but are extremely dangerous to your mental health, harmony, and prosperity. They are soul-crushers.

Soul-crushers have let their dreams die, leaving them with nothing but jealousy, bitterness, and cynicism. They simply won't stop until they crush your soul. Some of these soul-crushers do this because they are your "friends" and they think they're saving you from yourself. You need friends like this like Boeing needs a screen door on a 777. Some of these people try to crush your soul because they are *not* your friend. They will ridicule your aspirations and even try to sabotage your results, because if you become successful, happy, and prosperous – you take away all of their excuses as to why they haven't done the same. In either case, you've got to detach from these people as rapidly as possible.

You can try and drift away in a gradual, unnoticed way. Or sometimes you might need to tell them, "I love you and want the best for you, but I cannot allow myself to be around you any longer. Your negative, cynical view of the world colors everything you do, and I don't want to be infected by that mindset." You do not need more input from people who want to tear you down, tell you why what you're doing is a bad idea, or why it will never work. You have plenty already. Move on and replace them with people who bring more positivity to your life.

With all this in mind, take an inventory of the people you are spending a lot of time with, online and off. How would you rate their default setting toward money, success, health, and happiness? Are there people you need to release to create the new you?

Most people want to be surrounded by others who give them permission to stay the way they are. That was the old you. For the new you, strive to be surrounded by people who challenge you to become a higher and better version of yourself.

Having said all that, beware the messenger...

I sent an early draft of the manuscript to my friend Alan Weiss. He noted that my take on organized religion focuses on our being sinners and needing redemption. Then he went on to say, "*But that's exactly your point in the book.* You're telling us we're damaged and manipulated – often or usually without knowing it – and we need your redemption. The parallel is too overpowering to escape."

Guilty as charged.

I'm humble enough to believe that every person can make a difference and arrogant enough to speak up when I think I can be that person. The Biblical definition of redemption is usually accepted as the action of saving or being saved from sin, error, or evil. While I don't believe I'm a supernatural entity that can protect you against sin, I do believe I'm a smart enough chap to offer redemption from repeating the stupid mistakes I've already made. But you should evaluate everything I suggest with the discernment and critical thinking I suggest applying against everyone and everything else.

I don't write books summarizing the conventional wisdom on a topic. I write one only when I have a strong viewpoint on something. And this topic – killing off an older version of you and creating a radical rebirth – is one of those topics. I may have the diplomacy skills of an eggplant, but everything I'm writing you is my unadulterated truth as I know it. That doesn't mean I'm right. It's not my goal to tell you how to think about anything. It is my goal to cause you to think about an issue, question the premise, evaluate what I'm suggesting, and then come to your own conclusion.

Chapter Sixteen

The Power of Forgiveness

I **TOLD YOU EARLIER** that along with the balmy breezes and swaying palm trees, my relocation to Miami also delivered to me the gift of coming face to face with a hopped-up crack addict with a gun. That encounter ended up pretty much as you might think, with my taking a bullet to the gut.

Smart readers have probably already deduced that I survived. But that outcome was really touch and go for a while and involved some pretty heroic work by first responders and the hospital staff. The physical healing process wasn't easy. But it almost seemed so in comparison to the process of the mental healing. Fortunately, by this point in my life I had been exposed to some spiritual teachings that were quite helpful to me. These included the work of the good reverends Charles and Myrtle Fillmore and Catherine Ponder.

Forgiveness was a common theme in this work, and I set out to forgive my assailant. Believe it or not, I was able to quickly and readily forgive the man who shot me. I know what it is to be powerless over an addiction, so while I hated what my attacker had done, I could empathize with his lack of self-control and likely desperation.

The guy I had a real hard time forgiving – was the doctor who saved my life...

When I woke up in the recovery room, he told me that they had a hard time locating the bullet in my body but had removed it. Then he casually mentioned that as long as they were in there, they took out my appendix. That didn't make any sense, because I had been shot on the other side of my abdomen. He told me it was just standard procedure that whenever they had to open anyone up, they removed the appendix as a precaution. "That way you won't have problems later. You don't need it anyway."

I was incredulous at the arrogance and audacity of someone who would cut an organ out of my body without even asking me, and left the hospital with a great deal of resentment. To make matters worse, the surgery didn't work out very well. The sutures came undone, and I looked down to see blood all over my shirt one day. That necessitated another trip to the hospital. A week after that, the wound became infected, requiring another hospital visit. And the pain was unbearable. It didn't matter whether I was lying down, sitting, or standing, I couldn't find any position that relieved the agony.

As the months wore on, instead of getting better, I was getting worse. I woke up four or five times a night in a cold sweat. I had no energy, and my body seemed to be always fighting off an infection. This involved trip after trip to doctors and numerous tests. Along the way I had an intuition. I asked my regular doctor to take an X-ray of my abdomen, worrying that the hospital left the bullet inside me.

"Save your money," he chuckled. "They are crazy at Jackson Memorial, but not that crazy."

The next step was a visit to a gastroenterologist to have an entire upper and lower GI series of tests done. As I was getting ready, the nurse noticed my scar and inquired about the cause. I told her about the surgery for the gunshot wound, and she went ahead with my testing. About 20 minutes later, she came back holding up my X-ray and casually said, "I see they left the bullet inside you. Is that because it's located so close to your spine?"

Imagine my shock, then anger. I had been sick for months and months. I had no insurance and had spent a small fortune on doctors, tests, and specialists. And that doctor had actually told me they took the bullet out. How (and why) would he have lied to me like that?

I was very confused and not sure where to turn. I had malpractice lawyers lined up 10 deep to take my case. They all were telling me that an out-of-court settlement for a million dollars was a slam dunk. But this was after I had discovered the book *The Dynamic Laws of Prosperity* by Reverend Ponder. So, like I always did when needing guidance, I closed my eyes, flipped through the book pages, and stuck my finger in to select a passage to read.

It was on forgiveness.

In the book, Ponder discussed situations like being in a lawsuit with someone. She said that if you were suing someone, you must be holding onto resentment or revenge and couldn't be open to receiving all your allotment of prosperity. I saw my million dollars swirling down the drain...

But intuitively I knew what Ponder said to be true. I spent about 30 minutes meditating on the situation. I realized that while the doctors and medical team had taken out my appendix and left the bullet in, for whatever reason – they had also saved my life. I had arrived at the hospital on the doorstep of death. The EMTs had even needed to place a pressure suit on me in the ambulance because my heart was failing. The simple fact I could consider suing the hospital was because the entire team had kept me alive to even have that thought. They had done the best they could with what they had to work with and the consciousness they possessed.

I forgave everyone involved, released my resentment, and affirmed my tremendous gratitude for their service. And an amazing thing happened...

That night, I got a complete night's sleep without waking up in the middle for the first time since I could remember. I soon had another operation to have the bullet removed. But my health started improving dramatically the day I forgave, simply from the connection between thought and circumstance.

If you are holding on to revenge, love can't walk in. If you are hanging on to resentment, then you are

The Power of Forgiveness

hanging on to victimhood. And if you are holding on to victimhood, then there's no space in your mind to be a victor. You must release the negative feelings, as they only eat you up inside and prevent you from your good.

And after all you've been through, you're probably pretty pissed off. Don't blame you a bit...

Religions require you to feel subservient so they can control you. Governments need you to need them to remain in power. Millions of companies want to manipulate you to buy their product or service that probably isn't in your highest good. There are people who are jealous and resentful of you, working to sabotage you. There are people who love you and want the best for you – and they don't even realize they're programmed with their own limiting beliefs they're infecting you with. It's tragic but true. We have created a society that beats you down, infects you with fear, and programs you to be a worker drone in the collective.

It's understandable that you're angry with all of the forces and people who have been deployed to keep you down. It's understandable that you might want revenge. But the very best revenge you can ever achieve is evolving to create your radical rebirth. And that means forgiving everyone and everything that tried to hold back the old you.

You don't have time for vengeance or retribution, because they ultimately lead you to victimhood.

Besides, in most cases, the person who made or accepted the final decision was you. The only way to let go of victimhood and become a victor is to stop assigning blame to others and take responsibility for the life you're living. Maybe you didn't have the guts to accept your true sexuality. Or stand up for your desire to be an artist instead of an attorney. Or do the critical thinking necessary to discover your true path. Maybe you allowed fear-based people around you to dial down your dreams and you gave up on your true potential. Maybe you unknowingly allowed yourself to be programmed with low self-esteem and worthiness issues, so you subconsciously were afraid of success and happiness.

Welcome to the human race. We've *all* made decisions like this. We've all knowingly or unknowingly contributed to situations we say we don't want. That's what the mind viruses cause you to do. That's what causes all those other people to do the things they did to you. We're all prisoners in the Matrix, but the difference is, you've become conscious of that and made a decision to escape.

Forgive your parents and any others who may have influenced you to take a path that turned out to be the wrong one for you, because they were doing the best with what they had to work with. Forgive those who doubted you, ridiculed you, and attempted to keep you down. Forgive the politicians, religious leaders, tech companies, marketers, social media trolls, and even Milli Fuckin' Vanilli.

Forgive them all. Because letting go of the past, the hurt, and victimhood – that is the only way you're going to create your radical rebirth and step into your greatness.

You're able to read this book only because when I was that 15-year-old on trial for armed robbery, there was a public defender and a judge who both believed I was worthy of redemption. I'd like to believe I turned out to be worthy of that belief. One of the greatest gifts of humanity is our ability to forgive others and allow them the opportunity for redemption.

And there is one more person you have to forgive. Who do you think that is?

Exactly.

When I ask people in my seminars who is the one person they have the most difficulty forgiving, 99 percent say it's themselves. (And I'm pretty sure the remaining 1 percent are probably just too embarrassed to admit it.) This was certainly the reality for me.

Here's the most important thing to understand...

You know every bad thing you have ever done. You remember the time you stole two dollars from your mom's purse, you lied about who broke the vase, and you secretly had a crush on your best friend's lover. And you can instantly pull up every spiteful, lustful, and jealous thought you've had.

It's so damn easy to beat yourself up for the choices you made. (I know because I did it for decades.) You have to recognize that this self-flagellation and self-loathing is the result of years of the negative programming we discussed earlier. The forces that have been deployed against you – from government, organized religion, the education system and Datasphere – are mind-boggling. It's certainly no surprise that you're down on yourself and afraid you're not deserving of forgiveness. As Dan Millman points out in his excellent book, *Everyday Enlightenment,* you learned at a very early age two prime directives of being a human:

1. If you're good, you're rewarded.
2. If you're bad, you're punished.

These directives were drilled into your subconscious mind by your parents, teachers, babysitters, and coaches – and have been reinforced ever since by the Datasphere. They are indelibly burned on your hard drive. Making things worse, your perspective and perception are completely and totally fucked up. You honestly believe you're one of the few people in the world who has done bad things or had mean thoughts. In your mind, there are dictators, pedophiles, serial killers, and you – and everyone else is a philanthropist, Nobel Laureate, or saint. And let me share something that could be the biggest breakthrough you have this decade...

The better a person you are – the more caring, sensitive, and self-aware you are – the harsher you judge yourself and the more difficult it is to forgive yourself.

The irony is that those of us with the highest morals, standards, and values often have the lowest sense of self-worth and the hardest time forgiving ourselves. Because we fail to meet our standards on a daily basis. You believe the people you admire are faultless because they do a sweet interview

THE POWER OF FORGIVENESS

on the Jimmy Kimmel show or receive a humanitarian award. You think all your friends and family are noble because you're judging them from their virtue-signaling posts on Instagram. BREAKING NEWS: That shit ain't real. You think they're saints and you're a sorry sinner. But *everybody* does and says things they wish they never did.

The pope leaves wet towels on the floor. When Meghan is shagging Prince Harry, she is sometimes fantasizing about Harry Styles. Gandhi used to slam the door once in a while. At the Last Supper, Jesus had his elbows on the table. Buddha stole that milk and rice pudding from Sujata. Mother Teresa thought Johnny Depp had a cute ass. And Ellen DeGeneres once hit on Brad Pitt's girlfriend. (That last one is actually true.)

Yeah, you've done terrible things. We all have.

Give yourself a break. Forgive yourself. You, too, were simply doing the best you could with what you had to work with. And all of your journey – even the bad stuff, especially the bad stuff – can ultimately make you a better person.

Mistakes made you wiser...

Obstacles built your character...

Resistance made you stronger...

You're currently enrolled in the training program we call life. You're human, and humans make mistakes. Humans sometimes do things that are stupid, inconsiderate, and not nice. And we sometimes even do horrible things that result in horrific consequences for others.

As an addict and alcoholic, I was lying to and deceiving everyone around me, all the time. I made mistakes that killed businesses, which created cruel hardships for the employees and vendors. I was so insecure that, for the first 35 years of my life, I cheated in every relationship in a desperate attempt to feel attractive. I came to understand that no matter how bad I thought I was, I must forgive myself and move on, or I would continue to manifest a life of misery, limitation, and lack. Any time you fail to be your best self, remember that you're still a student – learning to live, love, and evolve to the highest possible version of yourself. Mistakes are part of the process.

Something I do every New Year, and sometimes even more often, is the "burning bowl" ceremony. This is a ritual where you release the things that no longer serve you and substitute them with new things you want in your life. It's a great way to begin your radical rebirth. Here's how it works...

Take a sheet of paper and draw a line to divide it in half. On one half, write down the things you want to release from your life, and on the other half write down the things you will replace them with. Example: You might release vengeance and replace it with forgiveness. Or you may release overeating and replace it with exercise. Or let go of revenge and replace it with love. #ProTip: The change you fight the most is usually the breakthrough you need the greatest.

Once you have your list, tear the page in half. Keep the half that lists the positive replacement choices you have made. You might want to tape this on your computer, post it on your dream board, or keep it in your journal or diary. It's powerful, positive programming for your subconscious mind. Then take the other half of the page with the things you want to release and burn it in a bowl. This allows you to let go of the limiting beliefs, poor choices, and wrong turns of the past – by figuratively and literally burning them up and letting them fade back into the nothingness from which they came.

You know why people like Gandhi, Martin Luther King, Jr., and Mother Teresa demonstrated such lives of prosperity, even though they had the same human frailties as the rest of us? They accepted their humanity and realized that it included both good and bad.

They forgave themselves.

And instead of forever punishing themselves for their failings, they changed the equation: Instead of dwelling upon their flaws, they celebrated their gifts and chose service to others. They broke the self-sabotage cycle and accepted themselves as worthy. They realized they had debts that could never be paid back, so they paid them forward.

And that's what you must do...

When someone comes to me, and his or her prosperity seems blocked, forgiveness is the first place we look. Allow me to suggest the following four steps for yourself:

1. Mentally forgive everyone you feel has wronged you. (If you have some people you feel moved to tell this in person, do so.)
2. Mentally ask for forgiveness from the people you have wronged in the past, gossiped about, or been in any other disharmony with. (If you feel moved to ask for this in person, do so.)
3. If you have accused yourself of failure, misdeeds, or mistakes – forgive yourself.
4. As part of your radical rebirth program, resolve that for any obligations you cannot pay back, you will find an alternate method to pay them forward.

Once these four steps are completed, the old you will die off and you're free to create the new one.

Chapter Seventeen

A Rebirth Worthy of You

WHO IS REALLY more arrogant – the believer who is oblivious to science or the atheist cynical of faith? It's undoubtedly a tie.

I get asked frequently why I'm so hard on organized religion. Most who ask the question believe I'm on a crusade to convert the world to atheism. In actuality, that's the last thing I want to do. There are many people whose faith nourishes their lives and souls in wondrous ways, and that's a beautiful thing to behold. Years ago, I was attending a Christmas Eve service at the Unity on the Bay church in Miami. The lights were off, with the only illumination provided by the candles 800 of us were holding while singing "Silent Night." I remember thinking at that moment that if religion was just some crazy shit made up by humans – it's was some pretty good shit.

I've often felt that I would be a much happier person if I could cry more often. My decades of anxiety, insecurity, and fear ingrained such a deep defense mechanism in me that it can sometimes prevent me from accessing the deeper levels of my humanity. I don't have the slightest idea whether god exists. No one does. It's an issue I think about a lot because it meets some of my criteria for favorite questions: Questioning a premise, you can't readily deduce the answer, and it makes my brain hurt. And the question leads to a never-ending series of additional questions.

The rational, logical, analytical, compulsive, addictive, controlling aspects of me rebel against the idea of giving away my power. I fiercely protect and defend the power to choose my thoughts and create my future. But truth is, there are moments for each of us when we desperately need to give away our power. Many former addicts point to the moment they recognized a power greater than themselves as the turning point in their recovery. At some point, all of us need to choose powerlessness – to voluntarily surrender our power and break down sobbing in the arms of another, allowing them to be powerful for us. For many people religion provides this outlet.

Tragically, I have more than a few friends who have buried their children. Most of them are strengthened by a belief that when their loved one left the earth, heaven got another angel. If that belief gives them the sustenance to move forward with their lives, why not celebrate the beauty in that? My fight is not with god but organized religion. The fight is driven by my desire to combat the two most destructive and dangerous beliefs religions propagate:

1. That you are not worthy to be healthy, happy, and prosperous.

A Rebirth Worthy of You

2. That your real life hasn't begun yet, and if you patiently slog your way through the warm-up, you'll be rewarded with your true life (and happiness) later.

It's like your mom promising if you eat your broccoli, you'll get dessert, and then after you choke down the green stuff, you find out she lied. There are millions of people unconsciously rushing through what they believe is a prologue to their life but is actually a prologue to their death. And there aren't many situations more tragic than a life not lived.

Make sure you live, really live, your life – the one you're in right now.

There are random acts, but no random lives. As you now know, your life (whether we're discussing the old one or the reboot you desire to create) is the harvest of the thoughts you give precedence to. And the daily actions those thoughts produce. While it may sound simplistic to some, the profound truth is that when you transform your thoughts, you can transform your life. The final and decisive step of this transformation is the release of victimhood.

Back in the day, I had the opportunity to have dinner with a high-achieving couple I admired greatly. I was a fan boy, eager to impress them with my work ethic, tenacity, and desire to become successful. I did what I always did in those days: regale them with story after story of the trauma, drama, and victimhood in my life. I complained about all the lazy ignorant people on my team, my health challenges, dysfunctional relationships, and all of the other unfair things the universe was assaulting me with at that point in my life. As we were leaving the dinner, the husband looked at me and quietly asked, "Randy, have you given any thought to what you might be doing to attract all of these bad things in your life?"

WTF! Did he not hear everything I had just told him? Was he so clueless he couldn't understand how unfairly I was being victimized? Or was he just a cold-hearted sonofabitch?

Can't remember exactly what I mumbled back, but pretty sure it showed I wasn't buying into his woo-woo, New Age bullshit. But his question had me grinding my molars for weeks. The sheer inexplicability of his not feeling sorry for me forced some deep introspection.

When you're doing self-examination, the best results usually come when you ask questions of self-discovery. Not tepid cliché questions, but radical self-inquiry. This type of question moves the focus from external factors to internal ones. External focus is designed for you to escape responsibility, play victim, and blame others, while the internal questioning is where the breakthroughs come from. This process led to the most important question I have ever asked myself. As I reflected on the numerous health challenges, multiple business failures, and my 11 negative, dysfunctional relationships in a row, I asked…

Was there one person who was always at the scene of the crime?

I didn't like the answer I got. But that was the solution that set me free. The realization that I had lived in a victimhood mindset my entire existence created the escape. Looking back on that dinner now, I can recognize my whining for what motivated it: my full-time job as a professional victim. These stories of trials and tribulations I habitually trotted out were an almost prerecorded "data dump" I did anytime someone asked about me. It was my desperate subconscious attempt to overcome my low self-esteem and feel worthy.

The right question blows up your "story" – the victim narrative you've created to avoid facing reality and personal accountability. Once you get this, you change your perception of life and see yourself as a co-creator, not a recipient. Instead of looking for other people and circumstances to blame, you direct your attention internally – to what you must change to become the person you want to be and live the life you desire to live.

Unfortunately, this process will likely also expose one final tripwire along your path...

Because when you decide to stop being a victim, your "inner victim" is going to fight like hell for survival. To really kill off this part of the old version of you, *you have to* uncover *the payoff you get from being a victim.*

Very few people possess the self-awareness to see their circumstances objectively. Many believe they are innocent victims and would never think to analyze what they might be doing to contribute to that situation – and the emotional reward they're getting from being in it. At its ultimate level, everything in the universe (including you and me) is vibrational energy. And energy can be attracted or repelled. We all know certain people who are magnets for attracting victim energy. It's simple physics...

When the victim is ready, the crisis will appear...

You might wonder how I'm so certain of this, since I have no training or education in the science of physics. That's because I don't need it. I earned a Ph.D. in victimhood. In fact, I spent the first 30 years of my life attracting calamity after calamity.

In my case, I was an emotional cripple unable to accept love, so I substituted attention and sympathy in its place. Without boring you with all the specifics, the bottom line was simply I attracted disasters, calamities, injustice, illness, accidents, and other misfortune, because it provided an emotional payoff. And the more failures, dramas, and obstacles I encountered (read "created") – the more attention and sympathy I received. This generated a feedback loop of drama, trauma, and dysfunction.

And that's the power of the dark side of victimhood...

You think you're being victimized (and sometimes you are), but in addition, you are receiving rewards you perceive to be greater than your victimization. So, on a subconscious level, you take behaviors that attract more mayhem and misfortune into your life. Your life then spirals down to the desperation point. You're forced to make a choice between being a victim or being a victor. Sadly, too many people choose victimhood. The end results are ugly and usually involve addiction, abuse, suicide, or death by another cause. You keep pursuing that emotional payoff in ever-increasing highs until you overdose and there are no more payoffs.

Being a victim might make you feel noble or spiritual – the little guy or gal fighting the forces of evil. Or like me, you can become desperate for the attention and sympathy, afraid to lose it. But what you perceive as payoffs for victimhood aren't real. They're a self-created prison cell. How does this play out? Let me count the ways:

- ▶ Starting arguments with your spouse to create drama.
- ▶ Abusing food, alcohol, or other drugs.
- ▶ Accepting lower wages or exploitative work situations.
- ▶ Settling for negative, dysfunctional relationships.
- ▶ Vegging out with TV or *Fortnite* five hours a day.
- ▶ Walking away from lucrative opportunities.
- ▶ ...and literally hundreds of other scenarios.

You can get quite high on the supply of being a victim. But there's a much better high...

Being a victor.

You don't re-create yourself and live a prosperous life because you have no challenges. You create a prosperous life by seeking out a continuous progression of escalating challenges – then doing the difficult work of trial and error, growth, and self-development to overcome them.

Until now, our discussion has been about the thinking process: the thoughts you allowed yourself to be influenced by (whether consciously or subconsciously), the beliefs they caused you to develop, and then what the results of holding those beliefs have been. This introspection and the accompanying critical thinking are important work – because they allow you to become conscious of the process, then mindfully direct it in a positive manner. This is the method that creates a radical rebirth. That rebirth is going to bring you face to face with some central, existential questions.

The meaningful questions at this point in your journey become:

- ▶ What would an average day in your new life look like?
- ▶ What goals would cause you to throw the sheets off every morning and jump into your day? And most importantly,
- ▶ Who do you want to become?

The goals you set for yourself become essential building blocks for the ultimate vision you craft for your radical rebirth. Perhaps both the perils and potential of selecting the right goal are best demonstrated by Ted Kaczynski, a/k/a the Unabomber. Most people know him only as the crazy guy who lived in the wilderness mailing pipe bombs to professors and tech people in a futile attempt to get humanity to destroy technology and start all over again. Would it surprise you to learn that Kaczynski was a child prodigy who was accepted to Harvard at 16 years old and went on to become a Ph.D. and a professor himself? He was eventually captured after a manifesto he wrote was published by some major newspapers at the request of the FBI. You might expect that this manifesto would be crazy, and primarily it was.

Yet the manifesto also demonstrated his critical thinking ability and contained some intriguing ideas. Kaczynski stated that for people to be truly happy, they require challenge – most specifically to have goals which require serious effort. In the manifesto he divided goals into three buckets:

- ▶ Easily attainable goals
- ▶ Difficult, challenging goals
- ▶ Impossible goals that can never be attained

The overriding theme of his manifesto was that the hardest goals – the difficult problems the world needed to solve – were already accomplished. The only goals left were the easily attainable ones and the ones impossible to attain. So in his eyes, there was no real meaning or fulfillment in life, no reason to continue.

I don't agree with Kaczynski's conclusion that all of the difficult but possible goals for the world have been reached. But I think a lot of people are in a similar place he was, especially in regard to the goals and meaning within their personal lives. They believe that the worthy goals remaining in their own lives are impossible for them to attain, so they've given up on their dreams. They believe that they will never get in shape, find true love, become wealthy, etc. Because they don't see breakthroughs happening, they stop experientially living life and have relegated themselves to simply existing through it. (Or for the believers, have decided this life doesn't matter because the real one is their afterlife.)

The number of people suffering from depression is mind-boggling, and the suicide rate is beyond alarming. Literally, billions – with a "B" – of people are self-medicating with drugs, alcohol, food, Tik-Tok, and Netflix. But these behaviors are only diversions that prevent us from seeking the true answers. I believe an important part of the solution is for people to seek out challenges worthy of them. People who are eager and excited by a challenging project have no time or proclivity toward depression. It's the people who are merely keeping their head below the cubicle, waiting out the week until Friday who are the likeliest candidates for depression, escape, or suicide. If you believe your greatest years are behind you, it's difficult to think your life is very meaningful. I've fought my own grueling war against depression over the years, but never when I was launching a new project or writing the next book I was excited to share with you.

There is no debate that Kaczynski took a horrific approach. But his ideas about goals and challenges are worth pondering. What's the default setting on your path in life now? Do you see your best years and work behind you or in front of you? Are you seeking new challenges? And are these challenges worthy of you?

As you map out the criteria for the goals, dreams, and yes, challenges of your radical rebirth, be mindful of how motivating they will be to you. Some goals are aspirational and/or inspirational. But while inspiration can be created by an external influence, motivation must be developed internally. Motivation is what causes you to act. For a goal to create internal motivation (read make a difference in your behavior), it must meet the following two criteria:

- ▶ Be achievable enough that you believe you can attain it.
- ▶ Be compelling enough that it motivates you into action toward achieving it.

If you're earning two dollars a day at a sweatshop in Asia, and you set a goal to be a millionaire next month, your subconscious mind is unlikely to believe in that possibility and act on it. Likewise, if you're earning two dollars a day at that sweatshop in Asia, and you set a goal to earn an extra four cents a day next year, that's probably not compelling enough to motivate you into tangible action to achieve it.

To create a radical rebirth requires bold, daring, and adventurous goals. The allure of these goals pulls you toward them and, in the process, forces you to become more. This starts an ongoing sequence of growth and development. Your next goals are set higher, and you evolve yet higher, creating an endless progression that leads to becoming the highest possible version of yourself. That's where the magic is, because setting goals worthy of you ultimately creates a new life worthy of you. Apply this same principle to the vision for your radical rebirth. It must nestle into the sweet spot between an outcome enticing enough to pull you toward it and the belief that you can attain it.

If your new life is not bold, daring, and a little frightening – what's the point in creating it?

You know the life you fantasize about when you gaze out the window? Live *that* life! Funny story: I was doing a seminar in Panama and my friend Erick Gamio was in the audience. His mother-in-law, who happens to be a psychologist, was with him. About halfway through my program she asked him why he hadn't told her I was a psychologist too. He assured her I wasn't a psychologist, psychiatrist, or anything like that. As the talk continued, she insisted he had to be mistaken because the information I was sharing about human behavior and motivation could be known only by a top mental health professional. She was gobsmacked when he told her that instead of being a mental health professional, I was actually a high school dropout.

When Erick recounted the story to me later, I could only laugh, because that's a common reaction I get from mental health professionals. I know more about human behavior – what causes the human animal to react and why we react that way – than any mental health professional on earth. Allow me to explain...

I spent the first few decades of my life as a neurotic, fear-based, and insecure guy, apprehensive of everyone around me. I ran every potential statement I made through a preliminary check on a computer screen in my mind, trying to predict if it would offend anyone or subject me to ridicule. I built a wall to protect me emotionally and was petrified to meet new people or go to events where I didn't already know everyone. I would even slow down to let elevators with people on them depart so I could catch the next one and not have to worry about making small talk with others. When you're this insecure, you're constantly studying everyone around you, wondering how to act so they will like you.

As an addict, your life revolves around lying to, deceiving, and manipulating people. You might need to borrow money for a fix or need an excuse to cover why you can't do your job. I did drug deals in half the crack houses in the Liberty City, Overtown, and National City neighborhoods. When you're dealing with heavily armed drug dealers, street hustlers, and gangbangers – you either become an expert at reading people or become a crime scene investigation.

Later I took all my skills and experiences – from dealing dope, running rackets, buying crystal meth, lying, cheating, stealing, and manipulating – and applied them as a marketer. I built teams with tens of thousands of people for direct selling companies, became a kick-ass copywriter, and excelled at Internet marketing. Fortunately, my motivations had become a lot more honorable and my morals had been developed. But the one constant in my two worlds – good versus evil, legal versus illegal – was my ability to gauge human nature. If you're ever presented conflicting theories on human behavior, and you must choose between 27 double-blind research studies of 20 million people conducted by the psychology departments of Stanford, UC-Berkeley, and Harvard – or me – bet the rent on my street experience.

I don't tell you all this to puff up my street cred. That world is long behind me and I'm ashamed to admit to most of it. I tell you in the hopes you'll understand the value of what I'm going to tell you next. Which is the single, most insightful lesson you'll ever learn about living a prosperous life. And it is this...

You don't manifest prosperity to the degree you are worthy of it. You manifest prosperity in direct proportion to the degree *you believe* you are worthy of it.

No more. No less. In exact proportion to what you believe you deserve. That's why your mindset is so important. It's why you have to police your subconscious mind, take charge of your programming, and work to continually nourish your self-esteem. Because every day of your life you must wake up and subconsciously answer the following question:

How much joy, happiness, and prosperity can I possibly put up with today?

It doesn't serve you to be timid, dream small, or settle for mediocrity. Because you are choosing to create a radical rebirth – to gestate and deliver a life that is worthy of the unique, powerful, and beautiful being you are – *and who you are meant to become.*

Live your truth, not anyone else's. As you embark on your radical rebirth, you're going to encounter a storm for the ages. Both the people who care for you and want the best, and the people who are jealous of you and want the worst, are going to agree on one thing: That what you're attempting is risky, perhaps foolish, even dangerous. They will want to warn you and protect you from yourself. You are quite likely to have many people caution you to "Watch out for the storm."

When they do, reach out and take their hands into yours. Hold them in light and love. Then gaze deeply into their eyes and say,

"I am the fucking storm."

Recognizing Generosity

IN NO PARTICULAR order, my grateful thanks to...

Prince, Alicia Keys, Jonny Lang, Camila Cabello, Jimmy Buffet, and Coldplay, the artists whose work provided the soundtrack to my life, or at least the part of it spent birthing this book.

Steven Pressfield, Ocean Vuong, Harry Chapin, Andrew Sullivan, and Trevanian, the writers who intimidate me with your genius. As I review my own prose, you almost make me delete mine for being garbage. But your work inspires such a desire to create that I don't.

Bob Burg, Bob Negen, Art Jonak, and Jaime Lokier for reading this early on in manuscript form. Their sage advice and input made this book a better resource for you.

Alan Weiss, who read the manuscript and refused to endorse it. He felt it contained blind hate, unbridled animosity toward religion, and cast aspersions on believers. Alan was right, and that really wasn't my intent. Hopefully, his input improved the book from judgmental and condescending to merely obnoxious and threatening.

Vicki McCown, who edits with the precision of a brain surgeon, the blade of a ninja, the wisdom of a goddess, and the heart of an angel.

Ford Saeks, Amanda Martin, and the crack commando team at Prime Concepts Publishing for getting this book into the wild.

Christopher Hitchens, David Bowie, H. Emilie Cady, Richard Dawkins, Marc Andreessen, Jeff Bezos, Naval Ravikant, and Bruce Lee – for being the thinkers of the thoughts who make me think about my thoughts.